LOMA LINDA UNIVERSITY
HEALTH

Special thanks to the LLUSM Class of 1963 of which Timothy S. Greaves was a member. The class sponsored the writing of this commemorative book.

Of Courage, Compassion, and Endurance: The story of Timothy S. Greaves is also available for online purchase at <www.trafford.com> or email <orders@trafford.com>.

Most Trafford titles are also available at major online book retailers.

Of Courage,
Compassion,
and Endurance

The Story of
Timothy S. Greaves, MD

❧❧❧❧❧

By Dorothy Minchin-Comm
2013

Order this book online at www.trafford.com
or email orders@trafford.com

Most Trafford titles are also available at major online book retailers.

Printed in the United States of America.

ISBN: 978-1-4669-8045-7 (sc)
ISBN: 978-1-4669-8046-4 (e)

Library of Congress Control Number: 2013902359

Trafford rev. 02/08/2013

Trafford.
PUBLISHING® www.trafford.com

North America & international
toll-free: 1 888 232 4444 (USA & Canada)
phone: 250 383 6864 ♦ fax: 812 355 4082

Frontispiece

Upper Left. Timothy S. Greaves graduates with a BSc in chemistry, Emmanuel Missionary College (now Andrews University) 1957.

Upper Right. Timothy S. Greaves graduates with an MD from Loma Linda University, 1963.

Inset Left. A smiling Tim (right) graduates from college in 1957. The entire world lies open before him.

Inset Right. On this day, Tim receives congratulations from his wheelchair. What will the future hold for him now?

Only six years elapsed between these two graduations. The ambitious, "all-systems go" youth on the left, however, has become the thoughtful man on the right. In his pensive eyes, we read the ravages of pain and a knowledge of life that has been inordinately heavy for his twenty-seven years.

Table of Contents

It's All in a Name

When Tim Greaves burst in upon the lives of his parents, Eric and Evelyn, in Bridgetown, Barbados, their world would never be the same again.

Full of energy and smiles, their bright first-born son was named Timothy. Being Bible students, they knew that the Greek meaning of his name, *Timotheos*, meant to "honor God."

He would certainly do that, but in ways that no one could have predicted. Nor could the family foresee the ironic meaning and strange significance that lay embedded in his surname, Greaves.

In thirteenth century Old French, and later in Middle English, the word *greve* meant "shin armor" for warriors. The oldest known reference to this protective covering—from ankle to knee—appears in the Bible. In the inventory of the armor of the Philistine giant, Goliath, we find his "greaves of bronze" mentioned (I Samuel 17: 5-8).

At first, Tim's sturdy, "well-greaved" muscular legs carried him faultlessly around the sports fields and down racetracks. Also up and down stairs and through university halls.

Then came the road accident that left Tim a quadraplegic. No kind of physical greaves could sustain his paralyzed legs any longer. For many months, he fought for his very survival, overcoming crushing disabilities.

In doing so, he put on the rich emotional and spiritual armor that enabled him to reconstruct his life and move on to a productive career.

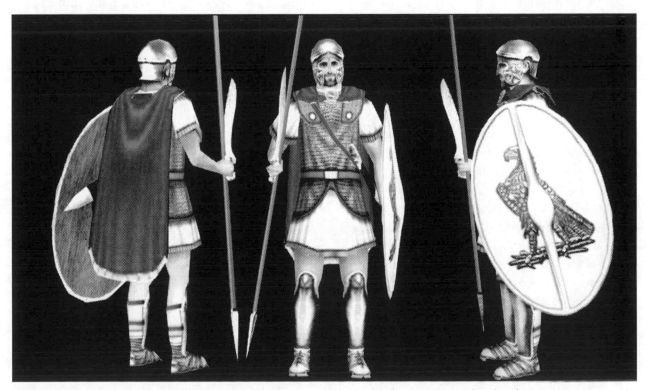

A Roman soldier displays full armor, including greaves on his legs. Anciently, this leg armor was made of a variety of materials—metal, leather, and fabric. Sometimes greaves were highly decorative.

Foreword

By Richard H. Hart, MD, DrPH
President, Loma Linda University Health

A boy from the "islands." A once-in-a-lifetime chance to attend Loma Linda University. Unspeakable tragedy. Undying love. And a career to be envied. This is the legacy of Tim Greaves.

Dorothy Minchin-Comm has woven this story of dreams, accomplishments, challenges, and doubts into a fascinating story of academic hurdles, cultural commitment, and protracted love. From Tim's early years in Barbados to his college time in Trinidad, and his eventual career at Los Angeles County Medical Center, this is a story of stubbornness and determination, frustration and dreams realized.

From childhood, Tim and Thelda survived years of separation, perceived slights, and insurmountable barriers. Eventually, it became an inseparable love that carried them through life. If this book told nothing more than that love story, it would be worth the read. But when love is compounded by challenges most of us can't even fathom, it becomes something very special. Truly, this is more than the story of Tim Greaves. It really is the story of a wife and family who realized their own values through his dreams.

The hurdle of medical school is tough under the best of circumstances, but Tim Greaves, rendered a quadriplegic during his sophomore year from a tragic car accident, came back with a determination to succeed. With the critical help of a determined mother, a dedicated panel of friends, and an indomitable will to move on with life, Tim tackled each step with freshness and determination. In the end, he became the first quadriplegic to graduate from a U.S. medical school. He credits his faculty and classmates from Loma Linda with giving him both the chance to try and the support to succeed. Even now, after his illustrious career as a cytopathologist, many remember Tim for his personality and commitment to excellence. With a keen eye for cellular changes, he diagnosed cancer and other diseases with the same precision in which he lived his life. His clinical skills live on in those who trained under him, including faculty now serving at Loma Linda.

Many of us watched Dr. Greaves' life from a distance, wondering at the challenges that he and Thelda faced every day. They attended alumni events, participated in church activities, traveled widely, and confronted their doubters every step of the way. I was personally blessed and encouraged to see them visit the Loma Linda campus year after year, a testament to their commitment to this University and all it represents.

Loma Linda University is proud of Tim Greaves for demonstrating our values and commitment to service. He epitomized the concept that "to make man whole" does not apply only to those who are healthy of the body, but to all those who maximize their talents in service to others.

Thank you, Tim. You left us all a legacy to emulate.

Preface

Herman Rickets, MD
Associate clinical professor of medicine
Loma Linda University
Director (retired), cardiology training
White Memorial Hospital

This is the story of my friend, Tim, a man whose memory I treasure. The two of us used to think that 1935 was a good year. In January, he was born, and I followed in December. Together, we began and ended the year.

Leaving our island homes in Barbados and Jamaica, we both started off at Emmanuel Missionary College (now Andrews University). A very cold place! As we studied, we stayed warm in handouts from the Dorcas Society.

Back there in the mid-1950s, the Civil Rights Movement surged toward a high tide. A vibrant young man, Tim knew everyone and wanted to go everwhere. He kept himself in the middle of everything.

Then it happened! A life-changing road accident transformed Tim into a quadriplegic. Like Job's friends, we all had immediate questions. What would happen to Tim? Why Tim? Who is going to care for him?

As for me, I had to wonder what would have happened if I had accompanied Tim to Los Angeles that night. I had planned to go with him on the "maiden voyage" of a new-old car he had just bought.

Here Dorothy Minchin-Comm explores the answers to these questions. The story expands upon the circumstances that blended to support an unusually resilient person.

We called him the "wheelchair doctor," the scientist, and the professor. Although on different paths, Tim and I lived our lives in parallel. We received our post-graduate training in the same institution, practiced in the same city, and made our homes in South Pasadena, California.

Meanwhile, curious questions arose. What might Tim have done had he not been injured? For one thing, he would have been an internist. He told me so. As for the rest, who knows? Could he have retained his strong faith and purpose to serve God and man? Would he have returned to serve his people in the islands? Maybe. Might ambition and materialism have derailed his life?

I know one thing for certain. He became the embodiment of Loma Linda University's motto, "to make man whole." Of course, Tim was not whole physically. He never *could* be.

Nonetheless, he chose his life mission to be the making of life whole in countless other ways. His legacy will last.

Dedication

To the many people whose expertise, support, and loving care enabled Tim to create a useful and fulfilled life for himself.

And to all of the others who have been disabled physically, emotionally, or spiritually.

On behalf of these—and more—Dr. Timothy S. Greaves would have consented to share his life story.

Distinguished Honored Alumnus Award

On March 4, 2013, during the Loma Linda University School of Medicine Alumni Postgraduate Convention Gala, Timothy S. Greaves received the coveted Distinguished Honored Alumnus Award.

The award is given by the LLU School of Medicine Alumni Association to alumni who have distinguished themselves in their field and personal life.

Honorees are selected for their contributions to medical education, medical mission service (both self-supporting and Church-sponsored), medical research, community service, government and military service, support of the goals and objectives of the LLU School of Medicine, participation in national and international medical and surgical societies, and commitment to and support of the LLUSM Alumni Association.

The award was presented (posthumously) during the APC Gala, held at 4:00 p.m. at the Ontario Doubletree Hotel.

The honored class of 1963, of which Dr. Greaves was a member, celebrated its fiftieth anniversary during the convention.

Introduction

A Tale of Four Hospitals

The story of Dr. Timothy S. Greaves needs to be told in the context of four hospitals. The first is **Loma Linda Sanitarium and Hospital,** the place where Tim received his medical training, forged his career, and made friends who became essential to his survival.

Founded in 1905, the College of Medical Evangelists (CME) graduated its first physicians in 1914. The school was renamed Loma Linda University (LLU) in 1961.

When Tim entered his medical training, he expected to finish with the class of 1960. The crippling accident occurred, however, and set him back by almost two years. Nonetheless, the College gave him the high-quality education that he so eagerly pursued. It also provided him with an internship and residency that launched him into his profession as a pathologist.

Not only did the institution care for Tim when he was first injured, but it also guided him into the long months of his rehabilitation. Above all, his classmates rallied around, enclosing him in a tightly bonded circle of friendship that would sustain him for the rest of his life. Things are

Loma Linda Hospital "on the hill" when Timothy Greaves became a student in 1958. Loma Linda University Medical Center opened in 1967 and is pictured above right as it looks today.

The oldest hospital in the United States, the Bellevue Hospital Center in New York City was established in 1736. It began with six infirmary beds in the Almshouse Hospital of New Amsterdam. The original facility was a psychiatric hospital. Today, it is a homeless shelter for men.

traditionally done that way at LLU—with compassion and commitment.

Second, we have the **Bellevue Hospital Center of New York University Hospital.** When Tim entered the Rusk Institute for Rehabilitation Medicine there in 1960, he received the best possible treatment available and was under the care of Dr. Howard Rusk himself, who had recently pioneered this branch of medicine by founding the center just thirteen years earlier (1947).

Founded in 1878, the vast **Los Angeles County Hospital** has dominated the crowded East Side of Los Angeles, California, for many years. The peaks and towers of this great mountain of concrete brood over a many-layered network of freeways, one of the largest and busiest traffic interchanges in the world.

During Tim's forty-nine years as a cytopathologist, he divided his time between this hospital and his professorship in clinical pathology and anatomic pathology at the University of Southern California.

Finally, we look at the **Community Hospital of Seventh-day Adventists** in Port-of-Spain, Trinidad. It is but one of many institutions that might represent Loma Linda's "dreams of medical mission." It is also an exemplar of the personal hopes and vision of Tim Greaves.

In many parts of the world, when young people go abroad for higher education, a common, reasonable hope prevails. After graduation, will they return to serve in their homelands? For a variety of reasons and because of the shifting sands of circumstance, the outcomes vary.

Tim never lost sight of his vision for serving in the Caribbean—not even after his extreme disabilities made it physically impossible for him to go home. One of the strongest expectations of his life was to establish a clinic of West Indian- and Guyanese-born specialists in Port-of-Spain to serve the Adventist hospital there. Although his initial attempt failed, today Loma Linda University sponsors the enterprise through Adventist Health International—along with some twenty-

Left. Known as the Queen's Park West Nursing Home, this somewhat fragile-looking Victorian house was a precursor of Trinidad's Adventist Hospital, yet to come. Three doctors—Robert Dunlap, and David and Doreen Bull—operated the facility in the early 1950s. Above. A *real* hospital appeared some time later. Under the auspices of Adventist Health International (headquartered at Loma Linda University), an additional tower has been constructed at the Community Hospital of Seventh-day Adventists in Trinidad.

six other hospitals and about seventy clinics in nineteen countries.

Because his Trinidad years nurtured him so well, Tim Greaves would have approved of the Port-of-Spain hospital standing as an exemplar of Loma Linda's mission outreach.

Together, these four hospitals set the stage for us to meet Dr. Timothy Sylvester Greaves. We go first to Los Angeles County Hospital. Within its sober white walls lies the strangely remote, often tragic, but all-too-familiar world of a great hospital. The patients who occupy the three thousands beds, and the medical staff who care for them, together, represent the whole spectrum of human suffering. At the same time and in the same place, one finds the best in scientific expertise that has been developed to cope with a myriad of illnesses.

Today, the department of cytology/pathology employs more than twenty-five technicians and researchers. Approximately 100,000 cytology specimens pass through these laboratories each year. A regiment of secretaries works steadily, typing, filing, and sending out reports to physicians

The Los Angeles County Hospital, where Tim worked as a research cytopathologist for nearly fifty years

throughout Los Angeles County.

On the sixteenth floor, a team of at least ten technologists works with the five surgical pathologists, who spend their working days studying the tissues and the smears.

Thus, they provide vital material evidence in the battle against disease.

Although their work has the impersonality of pure scientific research, still they live close to the heart of the human dilemma. One judgment they give will bring life and hope to a patient, whereas the next diagnosis will draw the darkness of dying and death around another. The range is infinite. The sputum test of the man who laid his life on the line and simply smoked his pack-a-day for too long. The enigmatic assortment of tumors removed from those many parts of the body where cancer is wont to lurk. Then again, the Pap smears that can play the more cheerful role of prevention. To be sure, surgical pathology and cytopathology are not without their drama.

What of the physicians who work at the hub of this important medical research center? You might have met one of them in room 16646, staff pathologist Timothy Greaves. He became the director of the School of Cytotechnology and a frontline researcher in the field.

Dr. Greaves spent his days in the laboratory, evaluating reports and preparing for his tutorials. He trained both medical and cytotechnology students. Even postgraduate medical doctors passed this way to receive further instruction. Tim stayed at the top of his game, a busy man. His telephone kept the world at his elbow.

Upon first meeting Timothy Greaves, one simply saw a pleasant, middle-aged man. He really didn't have the face of an obsessed, single-minded scientist. Not the kind of person some might associate with this kind of work. Rather, he had a genial, flexible face. One could imagine him laughing heartily at a party joke. Again, he could be sober with concern over another's misfortune. Or he might be studying intently and examining a critical issue.

One would note, too, the smart color coordination of his clothes—the brown tie, the apricot shirt, the tweedy trousers. Impeccably groomed from neatly trimmed side-burns down to the well polished, ankle-high boots.

But those boots never walked. They stood on the footrest of a motorized wheelchair. I looked again and saw the brace he wore on his right forearm. I noticed the metal hinge by which he activated his thumb and two fingers. Even though he might gesture to emphasize an animated thought, I realized that his arms were essentially useless. Those impressions remain from the first time I interviewed Dr. Timothy Greaves.

This doctor was a quadriplegic for fifty years.

Dorothy Minchin-Comm, PhD
Professor of English (retired, Emeritus)
La Sierra University, Riverside, California

From Left. Thelda Greaves, Tim Greaves, and Dorothy Minchin-Comm.

Over the years of their long acquaintance, the three friends usually met at the various Caribbean alumni events around Southern California.

Chapter 1

Programmed for Endurance

The place is quite unique. The first settlers named the island Ichirougnanaim (Arawak for *Red Land with White Teeth,* or coral reefs). We call it Barbados, and it the easternmost location in the delicate chain of islands called the Lesser Antilles.

Shaped like a well-carved mutton-chop, the island is tweenty-one miles long and fourteen miles wide. Unlike its fiery volcanic neighbors, Barbados is made out of an ancient coral reef. Instead of japed peaks, its 166 square miles of land rolls in soft, undulating hills. The rocky eastern shore faces the midnight blue Atlantic. The western beaches look to the more conventional sapphire Caribbean. Happily it lives outside of the regular "hurricane belt."

Politically, Barbados is the only Caribbean island that did not repeatedly change hands in the centuries of colonial conflict.[1] It has remained solidly British since 1625, now designated as a "Commonwealth Realm" and recognizing Elizabeth II as queen. Indeed, the island still cherishes its label of "Little England."

Timothy was born to Eric (November 19, 1906-September 11, 1999) and Evelyn Greaves (March 8, 1909-August 10, 2003) in Bridgetown, on January 16, 1935. A handsome, sturdy brown baby, he arrived full of confidence and a zest for living. As a pastor in the Seventh-day Adventist Church, Eric and his family would always be subject to change and travel. It "came with the territory."

The Greaves family traces itself back to the very beginning of Seventh-day Adventism in Barbados. It began with Tim's grandparents, Alfred Ernest and Albertha Adelle Greaves *(see family*

---

1 Barbados was first settled by the Lacono tribe of Arawak Amerindians. Following English occupation came centuries of African slavery, finally ending in emancipation (1644-1838). Independence ultimately came in 1966.

tree). They and their six of their seven children (along with a cousin) became charter members of the Checker Hall company. At first they met in a rented house. A year later (1927), up there in remote Saint Lucy, they numbered thirty-two members. Not a bad percentage, considering that the total Seventh-day Adventist membership for the entire island was only 267. (Today, the count is well over 16,000.)

Meanwhile, Wrensford Greaves, one of Eric's older brothers, owned and operated a family blacksmith shop at an important crossroads. It stood at the Mile-and-a-Quarter junction of Rose Hill and Bend Hill. Ever bold to talk of his faith, Wrensford happily argued doctrine with his customers as they came in. It was something that went along with the blacksmithing.

As the Mile-and-a-Quarter Church developed, Wrensford became first elder. His evangelistic endeavors were strongly supported by his younger brothers, Herbert and Eric. Dedicated in 1938, this church was known for sweet singing. People from all over the district loved to crowd around the windows to listen.

From his first day in the world, Tim Greaves grew up in a highly disciplined family. His grandmother, Christian Isley Johnson Boyce, had been the stoical matron who ruled over the family home in Cave Hill. Although a strongly spiritual and upright man, his father, Eric, was an intensely private person.

At the same time, Tim was a dearly beloved little boy. Ten years older, his cousin, Pretha Boyce, adored him and recalled him as a strong baby with wonderful chocolate brown skin. Although acne later scarred his face, that event was mere trivia compared to other challenges. Neither he nor anyone else made anything of that misfortune.

Left. The Greaves' family home at Cave Hill, St. Lucy, Barbados, looks to the Atlantic Ocean on three sides. Saint Lucy, Barbados, is the northernmost of the eleven parishes. Occupying only fourteen square miles, it is the most remote location from the capital of Bridgetown, St. Michael. Right. Almost any spot on the spacious property offers a memorable view.

Tim was a toddler when the Greaves moved to Guyana. The transfer would mold the boy's life forever. This moral compass that Eric and Evelyn Greaves had set for their son would have as yet, unthought-of influences in the future.

European adventurers had long quarreled over Guyana, that productive piece of South American property, rich in gold, diamonds, and sugarcane. After the Spanish and French had given up their claims, the Dutch moved in and called their settlement Starbroek, on the Berbice River (1790). Finally, the English arrived, took over, and named their capital Georgetown, in the name of their king (1815).

The Greaves moved directly to mission headquarters in Georgetown, Guyana. At first, Eric Greaves took charge of the colporteur (bookselling) work and the building of the Seventh-day Adventist mission in the capital. Since British Guiana (later renamed Guyana) is the only official English-speaking country in South America, the family did not feel undue culture shock in coming from Barbados. Indeed, the country is about the size of England, resting, as it were, in two "arms" of Brazil.

Three years later, after Eric was ordained, the family moved along the coast to the quaint old Dutch capital of New Amsterdam (formerly Starbroek). Their comfortable house featured both Dutch colonial and Victorian English styles.

For ten years, Tim remained an only child, learning to work through his childhood traumas and adjustments alone. Through the years, however, Mom Greaves took Tim home as often as possible to keep him firmly tied to his roots. Growing up in Guyana, he, of course, acquired a local accent. She did not want him to forget his *Bajan* (Creole/Barbadian) heritage. He didn't. Once the bond was made, it held.

His parents always stood nearby, guiding with a heavy hand whenever circumstances required. "My early upbringing," Tim would recall, "was nurturing but very stringent."

On one occasion, when he was about eight years old, he was at home in Cave Hill, head-high having fun with his cousins.

Two of them took Tim aside to induct him into the masculine rite of passage, learning to smoke. Huddled in the bushes, well away from the house, the boys tore up some brown paper bags. They rolled the paper strips so tightly that when they were lit they burned slowly enough to be a reasonable facsimile of a cigarette. At least the "cigarettes" didn't flare up in their faces.

The sheer quantity of relatives in the vicinity, however, led rather quickly to the discovery of the boys' secret activity. Tim's mother promptly gave him the biggest thrashing of his life. Then,

Left. The Greaves brothers were among the pioneers of the Seventh-day Adventist Church in Northern Barbados. The Mile-and-a-Quarter Seventh-day Adventist Church's recently dedicated church building is pictured here. Right. The next generation of Greaves cousins. Six of them surround Tim (son of Eric Greaves). From left: Radcliffe Hinkson (son of Ursula Greaves-Hinkson), Randolph and Livingston Greaves (sons of Wrensford Greaves), David and Philip (sons of Edgar Greaves), and Leopold Greaves (son of Wrensford Greaves). Seventh-day Adventism began in Barbados in 1884.

having suffered all of that, he was denied the chance to go the big family picnic. The episode marked him for life. Long afterwards, when he might have been tempted to try smoking with real tobacco, he had no inclination. "It was gone clean out of me," Tim declared. "Not the least desire remained. Missing the picnic may have been the worst part of the ordeal."

Tim was ten years old when little sister Norma appeared on the scene, followed eighteen months later by brother Donn. Family dynamics changed.

Tim cooperated and accepted the responsibility of being the model big brother for his younger sister and brother. They, in turn, adored him. Apparently his chief method of teasing them was to chase them down, hug them, and kiss them. The more they tried to escape, the more he smothered them. In sibling rivalries, all things considered, this mild kind of "abuse" appears to be the worst that he ever did to them.

In 2002, his colleagues from Caribbean Union College presented Tim with a memory album.[2] Norma Greaves' acrostic on his name, part of the album, was a whimsical tribute from a

proud little sister to her big brother.

> *Tells you the truth as it is*
> *Invites you over*
> *Makes a difference in your life*
> *Offers support*
> *Talks on the phone and enjoys it*
> *Helps you in whatever way he can*
> *Yells when he wants assistance.*

Mom Greaves had her own ways of building high principles into Tim's character. When he started nursery school in Georgetown, Tim had a nanny to conduct him to and from school every day.

When Tim was thirteen and living in New Amsterdam,[3] however, Mother announced that he should now keep his own room in order. None of the household help would henceforth provide any personal services.

Some days Tim managed very commendably. Other days he got into a hurry to run off to school with his friends. Indeed, he was constantly in a hurry. Always full of plans, he had plenty of energy to match.

2 Presented by the Southern California alumni chapter of Caribbean Union College, May 5, 2002

3 Tim Greaves' elementary schooling at Mission Chapel School was followed by Parkinson's High School.

Left. A sturdy, lively baby, Timothy joined the Greaves clan in 1935. Everyone, especially his adoring ten-year-old cousin, Pretha Boyce, fell in love with the "wonderful chocolate brown" little boy. Right. By the time Tim was one year old, his parents, Eric and Evelyn Greaves, had been transferred to work in Guyana.

One day the family helper appeared at the door of Tim's schoolroom. The boy might have been alarmed. He remembered, however, that this had been one of his "of-the-task" mornings. "Your mother wants you to come home immediately," the maid announced.

Eyes fixed on the floor, Tim struggled to his feet and dragged himself to the door. He felt every face staring at him. "So what's with Tim?"

The unspoken query burned itself into his tortured mind. He trudged home. What might his mother's intentions be this time?

As he entered the house, she did not so much as give him a glance. "You may go to your room and hang up your pajamas."

Back up in his room, he transferred the offending garment from the floor to the closet. Humbly and silently, he descended the staircase. "Now you may go back to school." His mother went on with her sewing and never raised her head to look at him.

His re-entry into the classroom caused further embarrassment. At recess his friends, naturally, wanted to know why he'd gone home.

As Tim told the story, he gestured helplessly with his braced arm. "How could I tell them that I'd gone all the way home just to pick up one piece of pajamas?" His eyes twinkled as he recalled the episode. "But I didn't do it again. You may be sure of that."

Tim loved the freedom of cruising around New Amsterdam on his bicycle. One day he found a *sakiwinki*[4] sitting on the roadside. He devoted an hour to teasing her. Having a biscuit in his pocket, he offered a piece to the little monkey. Repeatedly she reached for it with her tiny yellow hands, and he pulled it back. The game went on until he was tired. Tim got on his bicycle and went home, leaving the disappointed little creature where he'd found her.

A couple of days later, he passed the same way. This time, a masked bandit was waiting in ambush, big ears and round black eyes alert. *Sakiwinki* leaped out, fastened herself onto Tim's leg, and sank her teeth into him.

Knowing that he had fallen short of the highly ethical behavior that prevailed in his fam-

---

4 The *sakiwinki* (squirrel monkey) is native to Guyana. Weighing between one and three pounds, this delicate monkey is highly intelligent and favored as a pet. It has striking coloration—an olive-gray body and yellow limbs. Its dark eyes and black muzzle look out from a white mask below a distinctly curved "hair line."

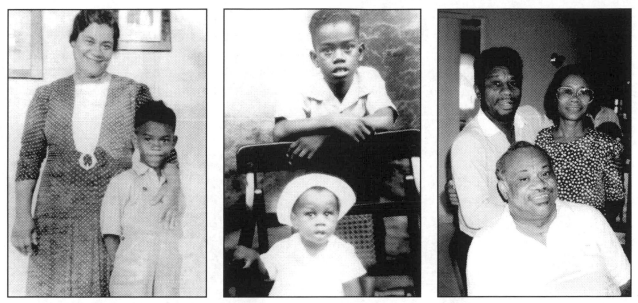

Left. For more than ten years, Tim remained an only child. **Center.** Suddenly Little Brother Donn arrived, having been preceded by Little Sister Norma eighteen months earlier. **Right.** Donn, Norma, and Tim remained a devoted trio all of their lives together.

ily, he went home to have his mother dress his wounds. And knowing that he deserved what he got, Tim offered her as little information as possible concerning the episode.

Occasionally, he fell into different kinds of misfortune. Tim well understood the three basic ground rules of the Greaves family: be frugal, excel, and represent the family well.

One day he cycled past the house of a lady he knew. Although a former member, she never came to church any more.

A large rock in the road threw him off balance, and he tumbled down into the dust. Picking himself up, he exclaimed in, as usual, a too-loud voice, "Oh, sh--."

The lady sitting on the verandah jumped to her feet. "I'll tell your father that you said that word!" she yelled.

Tim knew that, if this tale reached his home, it would be viewed as a rebellion against his father's gospel preaching. Sometimes, however, it seemed that almost cosmic powers protected Tim from some of his "felonies."

Suddenly, the distraught woman sat down, silent. She could carry her case no further. She knew that if she met Pastor Greaves, he would

The Eric Greaves family, New Amsterdam, Guyana. The occasion called for a group picture. Fifteen-year-old Tim was about to leave for high school at Caribbean Training College (now University of the Southern Caribbean) in Trinidad.

very likely be as concerned over her backsliding as over his son's swearing. Case closed.

Evelyn Greaves also had a great store of other ideas. "Son, you ought to be a medical missionary." She frequently threw out this suggestion: "Preach the gospel of Jesus. Teach and heal." His mother was a nurse, and the entire community benefited from "Aunt Eve's" loving care. Fevers, childbirths, pains of heart and head. She ministered to them all—with awesome managerial capability.

Tim learned high standards from both inside and outside of his home. Never—ever—was he to

settle for anything mediocre. Insofar as parents can lay down a life path for a child, Tim had a detailed preview of what his lifestyle would be like.

Above all, one profound, fundamental principle was driven into his psyche: you have a contribution to make. Do it.

Top left. Although he became a man of the world, Tim's roots in the old Cave Hill home never withered. He prized every visit that gave him leisure to sit on the verandah and love the landscape. Top right. Touring the grounds of Cave Hill in his wheelchair brought him right to the church that had been built on the land donated by his grandmother. Bottom. Thelda Greaves never wearied of the variety of scenery that tiny Barbados has to offer.

Chapter 2

What the Trinidad Days Did

Tim Greaves was only fifteen years old when he set off to boarding school for his final year of high school (1950). The fact that Caribbean Training College (now the University of the Southern Caribbean) in Trinidad was 400 miles from home in Guyana made no important difference to him. Located in the Maracas Valley near Port-of-Spain, the small school featured major turning points in the lives of its students.

Tim threw himself in the college's work-study program. No kind of labor discouraged him. At home, he never objected to cleaning the house and could polish the old wooden floors to a blinding shine. Later, when his parents built a house in Trinidad, Tim learned to make

His image bisected here by a pole, Tim Greaves worked at the College Press at Caribbean Training College. The work-study program allowed students to earn a good portion of their board and tuition.

bricks. Soon the young entrepreneur was making money on the side, selling them. He was always a "hands-on" fellow.

At CTC he worked at the College Press, a substantial industry. His workplace had four printing presses, a linotype, and a staff of about fifteen students. If running the ruling machine and the printing press was exacting, operating the old-fashioned paper cutter could be downright dangerous. One careless move could leave one crippled for life. Nonetheless, this whole experience simply added further discipline to what Tim had already built into his already rather remarkably organized young life.

One day Tim stood at the top of the stairs in the Girls' Dormitory. Athletic and opinionated, he was proclaiming—in a very loud voice—his views to a handful of his friends. He loved cricket and soccer, with tennis coming in third. He had energy enough for two ordinary boys. With his air of confidence and his talent for leadership, he was a kind of force of nature. His mother used to try to rein in his gusto: "Do, Tim, speak a little softly." To no avail. The boy was too much like his loud grandfather.

Down below, a little party of fifth-grade girls stood entranced, gazing up at the boys. The fact that they still wore "regulation British" short pants detracted nothing from their superiority. Thus, Thelda Van Lange saw Tim Greaves for the first time. His powerful presence impressed the shy child, to be sure.

Born in Guyana ("The Land of Many Waters," July 24, 1938)[1], Thelda Van Lange had arrived in Trinidad by a simple, seemingly random turn in family affairs.

Two years earlier, her mother's sister, Aunt

---

1 The British government had taken the colony from the Dutch. Thelda lived in the tiny village of Suddie where her father worked in the lumber business. The community was in the Pomeroon-Supenaam region on the Atlantic coast, one mile north of Onderneeming.

Amazingly, the old original dormitories of Caribbean Training College remain functional today, although they have exchanged their populations since Tim's time. Top left. Boys Dormitory (1978). Top right. Girls Dormitory (1978). Left. Porch of the Girls Dormitory, from which Tim made his loud and ultimately effective oration that caught the attention of little Thelda Van Lange.

Winifred Andrews, had come home for a visit. "Let me take Thelda back to Trinidad," she had begged. "I want her to be a companion for my two children. You still have four children left." The parents consented. They knew that she would have a solid Seventh-day Adventist upbringing, along with good educational opportunities.

Although the Andrews' home was only three miles from CTC, Thelda entered grade four in the government school in St. Joseph (the old Spanish capital). The next year, however, the college opened an elementary department. When school representatives came to recruit students, she transferred to the CTC campus.

Her uncle and aunt ran a tight ship. Uncle Centano[2] Andrews was better known as "Uncle Sim." As a young man, he took examinations to work as a telegraph operator with the Trinidad Railway System. He always refused promotions because they demanded that he work on Sabbath.

Thelda's Guaynese heritage is a colorful blend. Her great-grandfather was a Dutch planter. A black African line mixed with Jews (the Stolls) from Germany. Some Portuguese had drifted in from nearby Brazil. Perhaps the most exotic portion of her family line, however, occurred when her Scottish great-grandfather married a Guyanese Amerindian (*Arawak*) woman.

In 1594, the Elizabethan adventurer Sir Walter Raleigh (and others) came hunting for the lost golden city of Manoa and its King, El Dorado. (The Spanish, French, and Dutch had already fought over the attractive colony of Guiana.) The English landed in northwest Guyana in the area of Pomeroon. This event forecast the fate of the indigenous tribes in the Caribbean. European colonists found that neither the warlike *Caribs* nor the milder *Arawaks* could physically endure the labor demands laid upon them. The Amerindians in the islands, therefore, died out, and the African slave trade took root. In the northern crown of South America, however, they survived—and did so handsomely.

Among his classmates, Tim found a lively as-

---

2 Centano Andrews had been born in the year of Trinidad's centennial celebrations marking independence from Spain. Thelda joined her two cousins, Beulah and Vernon, in Trinidad.

An Assembly of *Arawaks* at Mahaiconi, Guiana, in 1844. (*Source: "Indian Tribes of Guiana," by W. H. Brett, 1868. Wikipedia Commons*)

sortment of new friends, including several cousins. Lloyd Stoll arrived with his brother, Kennard, and a dozen more young people from Guyana. They arrived on the Lady Rodney, a Canadian passenger-freight ship. Having slept in deckchairs instead of cabins, they reported a more interesting trip than Tim could. He reached Trinidad by air.

On campus, the boys slept four to a room. All were inducted into the work-study program. In the mornings, college students worked while high-schoolers attended classes. At noon they exchanged shifts.

While some freedoms prevailed, high school students were permitted no dating. College students partook of a few, very limited privileges. One day, a few boys overheard a faculty committee discussing potentials of romance among the students. "We'd better get outta here before we have to bury rocks," Lloyd advised. They scattered in great haste.

Nobody wanted to be sentenced to burying rocks. President Tucker (the predecessor of then president Percy Manuel) had devised this novel punishment for large infractions of the rules. The campus fields were full of rocks. It was not a simple matter of lugging them off to the side and—maybe—building a wall. No, they had to be buried at a prescribed depth. The hapless student had to do this without mechanical assistance of any kind.

Lloyd Stoll carefully avoided participating in clearing the grounds in this difficult and embarrassing way. He saved his nimble fingers to work in maintenance and repairs, where he earned the reputation of "Mr. fix-it." He also preserved his hands for when he (later) became a dentist.

Lloyd was Thelda Van Lange's first cousin, and he became one of Tim's lifelong friends. Born near the Essequibo River in Guyana, Lloyd liked to remind the fiercely Bajan Tim, "Man, we have islands in our river that are bigger than your Barbados, you know."

When Caribbean Training College was founded in 1927, it operated on the American system of education.

Upon the arrival of the new president, Percy W. Manuel, things changed. A Canadian, he held to his ambitious, home-born ideals of secondary education.

Also, colonial reasons caused him to transfer the college to the English school system. Along with other high schools throughout the British Empire, CTC students could then take matriculation examinations from Cambridge University.

This certificate came at three levels.[3] The standard was very high, and, at each examination time, many casualties littered the academic fields. The body count could be more than fifty percent.

Therefore, when Tim Greaves became the first CTC student to earn a grade one level pass in the Senior Cambridge External Exams, he became a campus hero, an accomplished upperclassman to be held in appropriate awe.

Throughout his life, Tim never ceased to marvel at "that little college." Most people love their *alma mater*, but, for Tim, the attachment was profoundly moving. "Do you know that maybe fifty percent of those students became professionals?" he would remark. "Often, those students came from the poorest of homes!"

CTC planted an essential motivation in the students. A truly great gift! Not only did they fulfill the hopes of their parents, but they also expanded their visions of what they could become themselves.

Tim never forgot the miles he and his friends

3 Senior Cambridge levels of passing: grade three, good; grade two, better; grade one, excellent.

walked and cycled to classes. "Nowadays, kids are just getting soft. They have too much stuff. Life is too easy." His face clouded with regret when he remembered the decline of the old work-study program. "I feel sorry for them." Then he concluded with a word of unadulterated wisdom. "For us, I think, achievement came more easily."

Being born into his little part of the old British Empire, Tim would have liked to train for medicine in Great Britain. Indeed, all of the countries to which he was connected were thoroughly British—Barbados, Guyana, and Trinidad. His Senior Cambridge pass entitled him to enter virtually any university in the Empire.

All things considered, however, he decided to enroll at a Christian institution, Emmanuel Missionary College (now Andrews University) in Michigan. There he found himself in competition with many other young people, just as brilliant and ambitious as himself. All were hoping to be accepted at medical school in Loma Linda, California. Not all who desired entry, however, were admitted. Not by any means.

Left. The kind Aunt Winifred Andrews, who became Thelda's "other mother" in Trinidad. **Right.** Thelda as a young immigrant in Trinidad.

The faculty and student body (smartly turned out in uniforms) at Caribbean Union College in Trinidad (about 1958). Among the faculty on the first row: Walter Kennedy (Print Shop and industries); William Osborne; Percy Manual (president) and wife Lou; Linda Austin (Spanish and dean of girls, long service); and John Dunnett (English) and his wife. Caribbean Training College changed its name to Caribbean Union College in 1956.

He was not alone at Emmanuel Missionary College. Other Caribbean students had gone before him, and more would follow. Between the busyness of classes and the warmth of friendships, Tim weathered the winters well. Indeed, he thrived.

One summer in New York, he found work at a nearby factory making helmets for firemen. Because he applied himself to his work with his customary zeal, he was offered a permanent, managerial job. The offer was a pleasing vote of confidence, of course. He kept his eye on his real destination, medicine. He intended to be—and was—the first physician in his family.

In time, his passion for travel made him acquainted with most of the northeastern states. Indeed, there scarcely seemed to be a city there that he didn't know about. To promote this par-

ticular ideal, he bought his first car. Most of the time, it was a fixture in Daniells Hall parking lot. The poor thing had not the strength within itself to meet Tim's plans for it. Often, for weeks, it sat dejected in a puddle of four flat tires. It was, however, as far as his money could go at the time.

"Man," he complained to Lloyd one day, "I'm just going to have to buy four new tires."

"Concerning your car, uh, Tim!" A thinly veiled undercurrent of cynicism came through in Lloyd's response. "Why don't you just sell the car, and then you can buy the tires you need." Tim held his peace. Some day, he decided, he would have a car that could function above such cheap scorn.

These transportation besetments notwithstanding, whenever Tim could drive somewhere, he avoided following the same route. "Why would

Tim's was the last twelfth grade graduating from CTC (1950). From left: Hector van der Pool (musician), Lucille Williams (class sponsor), Timothy Greaves (sergeant-at-arms), Cyril Clements (vice president), Bernard Benn (president), Leila Hardy, Ruby Carrington, Albert Pierre, and Dorothy Lewis.

you want to keep going the same way all of the time when you could see and learn new things?"

Tim Greaves graduated from Emmanuel Missionary College in December, 1954, with a BSc in Chemistry. By now his mother's seed planting had taken firm root, and the ambition to become a doctor filled his horizons. He was just twenty-two years old when he received that wonderful letter of acceptance to the College of Medical Evangelists (now Loma Linda University) in California. The road to the promised land of his career seemed to be leading straight away into the sunrise.

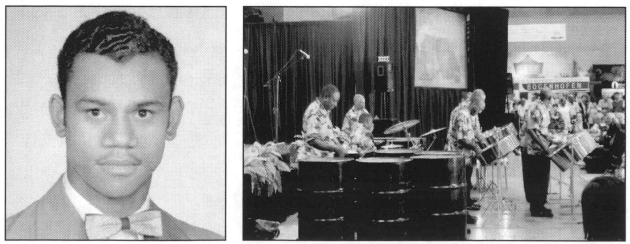

Left. Tim spent six months teaching at Bates Memorial High School in Trinidad. As soon as he gathered up a little extra cash, he was off to Michigan. Right. Still, his adopted country left an indelible mark on him. He never got Caribbean folk music and the native rhythms of the Trinidadian steel drums out of his system.

Chapter 3

Hitting Ground Zero

The first two years of medical school settled Tim into a professional routine of study, lectures, friends, and then more study and lectures. Although he enjoyed most of his classes, the mysteries of internal medicine fascinated him more than anything else. All of those elusive secrets that the human body could withhold and all of its complex interactions! He loved that challenge.

His keen sense of humor made him enjoy another rather therapeutic side of medical school. From the start, all freshman students, physicians and dentists alike, were required to survive one major, heavy course—anatomy. Spending an entire year with one dead body, of course, was a long, solemn commitment. Often, the pressure felt endless. The students worked in teams of four, two to each side of the dissection table.

Sometimes, however, relief from the tasks came in unexpected ways. For example, Tim's Jamaican friend, Herman Ricketts, worked alongside his lab partner, a girl. Their cadaver was female. To help lighten a little of the burden, Rick (as his friends knew him) started singing the song currently at the top of the hit parade: "Getting to know you. Getting to know all about you … "

At first the young lady in the lab team thought that the fetching and available medical student was singing to her! How disappointing to find that Rick was only serenading the cadaver.

With ease, Tim learned to maintain the balance between horseplay and the serious business of medicine. "Of course, I had all the usual adjustments," he said, "the ones you have to make if you're to survive in medicine." He remembered the deep involvement he felt with the patients. He retained that sensitivity all of the way into the pathology laboratory. "One has to learn to cope," he sighed. To cope indeed!

Tim recalled the first autopsies in which he assisted. "There was one lady I had seen for weeks. Yes, I guess it must have been months—if you count all of the times she was in and out of hospital. I always stopped to talk to her in the halls. It did us both good. And then … " He paused to study the triple rank of buttons on his telephone. "And then I went to assist in this autopsy. It was she. No one had told me." Even twenty years later his dark eyes still held the hurt. "I could hardly take it."

By 1957, three West Indian students merged into the company of alumni from both Caribbean colleges currently attending CME. First, Tim, a loyal *Bajan* (Barbadian) had arrived. Lloyd Stoll (from Guyana) entered as a first-year dentistry student, along with Linbrook Barker, another *Bajan*. Their history went back to early teen years in Trinidad. These and other university friendships were about to forge themselves into a veritable army of companions, all fiercely loyal to one another.

Medical school, to be sure, was demanding. Like most of his classmates, Tim struggled with the basic necessities. Just before the close of spring quarter in his second year, Tim bought another car. He determined that it should be at least a step or two ahead of the piece of junk he'd had as an underclassman back in Michigan. He found a 1951 Rambler Nash. A steel shortage resulting from the Korean War dictated that the car could have only two doors.

Enlivened by this new mobility and faced with heavy term-end examinations after the weekend, Tim decided to give himself a break. Friday morning, May 16, 1959, he visited his Bajan friends in Los Angeles, Dr. Cuthbert and Doris Arthur.

"Go with me, Lloyd. Take a day off." When his roommate declined, Tim canvassed others. "Come, man! Relax a few hours before the 'big time' comes." He had no takers, however, so he drove to Los Angeles alone. After all, the "new" car, such as it was, had suddenly given him unusual freedom. He just wanted to feel it for a few hours and socialize.

Late that evening, Tim rose to leave. "But why don't you spend the night with us, Tim? It's ten o'clock already." Doris Arthur pressed her point. "You can get up early and go back to the campus tomorrow morning."

When Tim Greaves could afford a car, he bought an eight-year-old Rambler Nash (1951). That model pioneered the field of compact cars. By contemporary standards, it looked lumpy and bloated and wore heavy fender skirts. Some called it a bathtub. Tim would drive his car for only ten days.

"Thanks. Next time, OK? I really can't rest with that heavy pathology exam coming up on Monday." He turned back to wave. "Don't worry. I'll have to take it easy. This Rambler's been losing oil, so I don't want to force it."

Thoughts of coming examinations continually stirred about in Tim's restless head. He had to get with the pathology notes. Dr. Gordon Hadley had literally left no cell unturned with his students. The National Board finals in pathology were coming up, and the professor was not about to let anyone be left behind.

Tim eased the Rambler onto Highway 10. Today, we have a transcontinental freeway; at that time, it was a four-lane, semi-country road. It wove its way east among fragrant orange groves and vineyards. On his left, the San Bernardino mountain range and old Mount Baldy shadowed the valley. Lame as his little old car appeared, he still loved feeling the pavement pulling away under him. It took no more than that to rouse Tim's innate travel-lust.

His memories abounded in sea voyages, clipper flights, and thousands of car miles. Especially he remembered home! Ultimately he'd go

back there with his medical expertise and set up practice in Barbados. Or perhaps Trinidad. Or even Guyana. That plan had embedded itself into the very fabric of his mind.

Then the signs for the Pepper Street turnoff into Colton came up. Almost back to his dormitory room. Tim twisted his head from one side to the other. Driving in the truck lane for forty-five miles had become very tedious. Still, he knew that the Rambler's uncertain health made any high speed presumptuous. One of these days he'd get a new car. The past week with the Rambler had disillusioned him. Was it really going to hold up for him or not?

Had Timothy Greaves glanced into his rear-view mirror just then, his eyes would have caught the reflection of headlights bearing down upon him. Coming fast. Very fast.

But he didn't.

Instead, the multi-moment of terror telescoped time for him. He felt nothing. The crash from behind wrenched the wheel out of his hands and threw him diagonally into the back seat. His head shattered the back window on the passenger side. His car careened over the bank into the scrub brush, and the "attack car" crashed down on top of him.

The other driver, an unsteady young man,

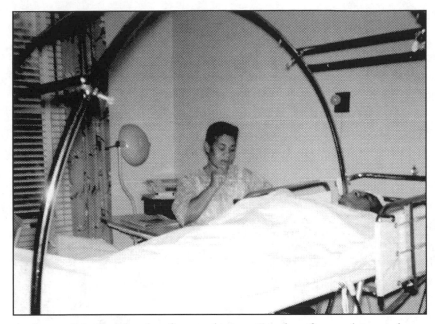

At Loma Linda, Tim lay for weeks in a Stryker frame, his mother keeping watch at his side. She had long hours to ponder the future.

drifted in and out of awareness. Doctors and nurses came and went. He knew he wasn't one of them. He was somewhere else. "I am the patient," he finally concluded.

Slowly, he began to assess his situation—in between the times that he kept lapsing back into stupor. The nasal tube was only part of his equipment. He also had a tracheal tube in this throat. The constant, crashing headache was due in part to the Crutchfield traction system in which he lay. The doctors had drilled into his skull and inserted tongs to hold the weights over the top of his bed.

"The fracture of the cervical spine is reducing well," Tim heard someone say. If anyone had told him that he would lie in this position for the next eight weeks, he could not have comprehended it. Not then.

As his mind cleared, Tim realized that he had a rather distinguished list of visitors. The qualifications of the doctors gave a rather clear clue as to the nature of his injuries. Dr. Kenneth Abbott, a neurosurgeon from Glendale Hospital, attended him. Also, two orthopedic surgeons at the medical school, Dr. Claran Jesse and Dr. George Wiesseman, plus Dr. Guy Hunt from the neurology department.

"What day is it?" Tim asked a nurse one morning.

"Tuesday, May 19," she replied. "You've been in and out ever since you were brought over here from San Bernardino County Hospital."

"San Bernardino County Hospital?" Tim slowly shuffled the ideas around in his heavy head. "What was I doing there?"

"They took you there after the accident." With deliberation the nurse checked the flow of the intravenous fluids. "When they found out that you were a Loma Linda medical student, they brought you here. We like to care for own, you know."

struggled drunkenly up the bank to flag down help. Deadly silence followed. The contorted mass of metal lay inert, the two cars locked in a terrible, twisted embrace. (Obligatory seat belts and headrests remained in the future.)

At six o'clock in the morning, Lloyd awoke to a firm knocking on the door of the dorm room. "Hah," he thought as he scrambled out of bed. "Tim forgot his keys and has locked himself out."

At the door stood the dormitory dean, fully dressed. "Tim Greaves has been in a very severe car accident!"

In that single moment, Lloyd entered into what would be a lifetime membership in Tim's support team. For starters, he went to the crash scene and took all of Tim's personal possessions out of the car, packed them in a box, and stored it in the dorm.

As for Tim himself, he remembered vaguely that, after the impact, a spotlight scoured out the inside of the car. "Hey, there's a guy in there—in the back seat." The voices floated down fuzzily from somewhere above him. Caring for nothing, he retreated into the dark, distant land of unconsciousness.

During the next forty-eight hours, Tim

She gave him a bright hospital smile and turned to leave. "We'll be in to turn your bed in thirty minutes," she promised. The Stryker frame had to be turned every three hours to prevent bedsores and to equalize blood pressure.

When pneumonia set in, Tim's case became potentially lethal. Immediately, however, a round-the-clock nursing team evolved. His cousin Robert Boyce flew in from Barbados. Mrs. Kennedy from the old CTC print shop days worked overtime shifts for him. His beloved cousin Pretha Boyce almost lost her own nursing job when she took off weeks to care for him. The hospital staff itself re-scheduled hours in order to give more time to Tim. He was not left alone for any hour of any day.

So the days drifted into one another. Class-mates came often. Even Hsein Ming Meng, the intern who'd checked him into the emergency room at San Bernardino that dreadful night of May 16. Tim looked forward to all of the visits. Piece by piece he began to gather up the fragments of his story.

The youth who had caused the accident had previously been charged with drunk driving. Sad-ly, he was still out on the street that Friday night. On top of that, the police in Ontario had stopped him for speeding just a few minutes before the crash. Thus, his fatal combination of (more) liquor and anger had brought Tim to disaster.

"I never looked into the police records," Tim later confessed. "I thought it better not to know too much about it. I didn't want to sue the boy or anything. I just wanted to save my energy for more constructive things."

With careful hospital etiquette, everyone judiciously avoided telling Tim anything more than he insisted on knowing about himself. He gradually came to realize, however, that he had not moved an inch since he'd awakened. From his neck down, he could feel nothing. Nurses and orderlies cared for his every need.

Two weeks later, Dr. Guy Hunt stopped by. Something in his wise, kindly manner gave Tim the courage to break through the tight-lipped medical secrecy surrounding his whole case.

So Tim asked the question. The great ques-

Tim worked out his physical arrangements to his own satisfaction and instructed caregivers on how to manage his motorized chair and all of its accoutrements.

tion that had now begun to fill his mind. "Doctor, I need you to tell me something."

Characteristically, he bypassed all the preambles. He had to know the facts. He didn't want a set speech, however well-meaning it might be. "Tell me, Dr. Hunt, am I paralyzed? I want it straight. What's the prognosis? Will I at least be able to use my hands? At least my hands?"

Dr. Hunt looked at him steadily and silently, estimating, perhaps, how to phrase his reply. "Well, Tim, we've done complete x-rays on you. Nothing was omitted. Your neck is broken at the C6 and C7 vertebrae. And ... "

"And that's very high, isn't it?" Tim's own razor-sharp mind began to put the answers to-gether for himself.

"Very high. Probably a transection of the cord at that level. Nearly all of the spinal nerves are affected."

"Will I get back the use of my legs at all? Or arms? Or will I always be a … a … a quadriplegic?" There. He got the word out.

"Always isn't a word that we like to use too soon, of course. But right now, the diagnosis seems pretty sure." Dr. Hunt briskly changed the immediate subject. "We'll get you into a rehabilitation program just as soon as possible. I've asked Dr. Russell Youngberg to work on this part of your case for us."

So the interview ended. The professor had said what someone ultimately had to say. And the student learned the basic facts for which he'd asked.

Timothy Greaves continued to lie looking at the ceiling. Hours passed. Attendants came from time to time to move him in the Stryker frame. His body responded like a lump of sodden straw. Could it still be his body? It felt like something entirely outside of himself. Did he really have to own it?

"If I look the other way," Tim wondered, "will the nightmare pass? Or is it always going to be like this?"

The answer was yes. He would not recover physically from the accident. Indeed, the doctors gave him about three months to live. Six at the most.

Still, a miracle occurred. He lived!

Eventually, the potentially incendiary question of Why came into the foreground. "If there had been no accident, what might I have been now?" Knowing his driving energy and ambition, some very conservative friends even surmised that the accident had actually "saved" Tim.

He was able to address the question quite rationally for himself. He recalled driving south after his first summer selling books in Western Canada. With him was a friend, who had been his partner for the summer. As they passed a marina near Vancouver, British Columbia, he looked at the handsome yachts riding at anchor. "One day," he remarked airily, "I'll have all of that too!"

Life without a wheelchair? Certainly there would have been differences. On one hand, Tim could even chuckle about what might have been. "Who can tell? Perhaps I would have gone bad. Become a dope addict maybe!"

Instantly, however, he dismissed the possibility and became sober. "I think I was aggressive enough and ambitious enough to have become somebody. Maybe a department chairman. I don't know." He flopped his hands into his lap. "Some of that energy now, of course, I must channel into just coping with the bare physical disabilities."

Would Timothy Greaves really have become an obsessed materialist? Who knows? "Well, that never happened." Tim concluded.

The many years he spent looking through his office windows, down upon the Los Angeles freeway system, in no way dimmed the dreams he held close to his heart. His vision of helping his fellow citizens of the Caribbean never faded. His ideal about making a contribution never wavered. That intention was so deeply ingrained that the likelihood of his becoming one of the conventional money-grubbing doctor-types that abound everywhere now seems quite remote.

In any case, Tim re-organized his life to accommodate his handicap. As he did so, a kind of spiritual miracle evolved. While the channels of Tim's vigor, strength, ambition, and potential changed, the adventures of his inquiring mind never stopped.

Chapter 4

The Fallout

Tim's mind raced through a vast, howling wilderness of despair. The outgoing youth who had just a few days ago thought he could conquer the world single-handedly! Where was he? Somewhere in this inert body that could do nothing whatsoever of itself? Or had that man gone away forever? A head upon a body that responded to nothing! What quality of life could be left for him any more?

In those early days of trauma, when he had to fight his collapsed chest muscles for every breath, he sometimes experienced terrifying moments when he could only gasp for air. When the Stryker bed was turned, he lived no farther from death than the space of a slim oxygen tube. He often believed that he must have reached the end.

"Still, I never really doubted." Tim nods his head slightly. "I somehow felt confident that I would live. Deep down, I was somehow convinced of that." The Twenty-third Psalm kept echoing through his mind, especially the part about walking "through the valley of the shadow of death." (Like many other disabled people, Tim always walked in his dreams.)

Tossed about in the huge swells of emotion and despair, his very desire to live sometimes waned. Then the core strength that his parents had built into him from childhood would rise like a sea wall around him. "It was this fierce conviction that God had work for me to do. So I had to believe that."[1]

After three months of intensive care at Loma Linda, it finally became possible to get Tim into a rehabilitation center. The Rancho Los Amigos Center in Downey, California, was nearby and convenient. Unfortunately, at the time, that facility was open to U.S. citizens only, so that left Tim out.

Now an intense search for an open door began. Any door.

At first, Loma Linda referred Tim's case to a physiatrist, Dr. Russell E. Youngberg (1925-2011, CME class of 1949.) At a time when rehabilitation medicine was still in its infancy, Dr. Youngberg had very recently opened the Reading Rehabilitation Hospital in Pennsylvania (1960).[2]

Recognizing that such an institution required a quiet, peaceful setting for both physical and spiritual healing, he and his cofounders, Drs. Irving and Marion Jones,[3] made a reconnaissance journey to a property that the Seventh-day Adventist Church had purchased in 1958. At first, the doctors thought that they were planning for an acute care hospital. Upon arrival, however, they realized that the real need in the area between Pittsburgh and Philadelphia was for a rehabilitation center. They rapidly shifted gears and looked

Dr. Russell E. Youngberg, co-founder of Reading Rehabilitation Hospital, with his wife, Dot

---

1 Andrews University, *Focus* (Fall, 1992), p. 30.

2 Along with his cofounders, Drs. Irving and Marion Jones (also graduates of CME), Russell Youngberg opened the Reading Rehabilitation Hospital, Mohrsville, Pennsylvania, in 1960. When the property was sold in 1998, it had 300 employees. (*Source: <www.adventistarchives.org/docs/CUV/CUV19980415-V103-8_C.pdf>*)

3 Drs. Irving and Marion Jones were in their residencies at White Memorial Hospital, Los Angeles, when they decided to join Russell Youngberg in his project in Pennsylvania.

at the twenty-six-acre Eberly Estate from a bold, new viewpoint.[4] "Stone Manor," the mansion, commanded a spread of twenty-six green Pennsylvania acres, in Cumru Township.

Coming from the broad perspective of having been born to missionary parents in India, Dr. Youngberg had developed a strong empathy for people. He believed that every life is worth living, whatever the circumstances. Working to make every patient attain his/her maximum level of usefulness became the passion of his life.

Nonetheless, the hospital was a bold adventure. Indeed, a leap of faith—a first within the Seventh-day Adventist Church. At the time, most rehabilitation facilities were geared to help polio patients. Reading Hospital, on the other hand, accepted any kind of disability. Even so, during the first two weeks that the hospital was open in 1960 (with 57 beds), just one person came to the door! A discouraging start!

Still, Dr. Youngberg declared that "God would find a way." Slowly, with great sacrifice and sturdy commitment, funds came in to pay for the purchase of the property, the remodeling, and staff wages. As Dr. Youngberg cheerfully explained the formula later: "Good people, hard times … and a happy ending! That's how it works."[5] He served as director of the hospital for the next twenty years (1960-1980).

The magnitude of Tim's injuries, however, set him beyond the range of treatment at the newly established center in Stone Manor. Forthwith, Dr. Youngberg arranged for him to go to the Institute of Rehabilitation Medicine in New York City. The facilities were located within Bellevue Hospital Center, the oldest hospital in the United States. No better destination existed anywhere for people with Tim's disabilities.[6]

Meanwhile, another consultant arrived on the scene. Although Tim did not meet Dr. Glenn G. Reynolds at that time, the two men had a memorable telephone conversation. In fact, their stories ran parallel in several ways.

In his third year of medicine, Glenn was working at his pediatric rotation at Los Angeles County Hospital. He still remembers the very date when it hit him—January 17, 1953. He contracted polio from a little patient in the wards. Although he survived, the ordeal left him a paraplegic.

Before he had time to even contemplate living in a wheelchair, a message came from the dean's office at the College of Medical Evangelists. Glenn's training would be terminated. Potential problems overwhelmed the decision-makers.

Shot down in mid-air, as it were—at age twenty-seven, Glenn lay there in his hospital, his legs inert and his mind spiraling down into despair. He pulled the sheet up over his damp face. How much could he endure, all at one time?

Then one of his friends strode in and yanked off the cover. "You do want to get on with medicine, don't you?"

Glenn looked up tentatively and whispered, "Well, of course."

"Then just leave it to us." In a short time, half a dozen of Glenn's classmates drew up a plan.

One morning, the delegation presented themselves to the administrators of the School of Medicine. "We see patients every day—and sometimes even doctors—in wheelchairs. They are quite able to learn in spite of their handicaps." The young men eyed their superiors carefully but very directly. "We think that Glenn Reynolds should be given a chance. All of us here promise to take care of him. We'll get him to his lectures and all of the rest of his appointments. We guarantee it. Please. Let him try." Their urgency to get Glenn back into school succeeded in reversing the administrative dictum.

---

4 Stone Manor was built in 1925 by a wealthy silk mill owner, Isaac C. Eberly, and sold at his death in 1958 (with 300 employees working at the time). By 1971, the center was bursting at the seams, and three years later a four-story modern facility (80 new beds) was opened. In 1979 an ancillary wing was built, followed by another three-story wing in 1985.

5 The *Columbia Union Visitor*, vol. 103 (April 15, 1998), p. 12. Dr. Youngberg opened rehabilitation centers in several other hospitals, including seven years of service in the medical school in Montemorelos, University, Mexico. Loma Linda University made him an Honored Alumnus in 1975.

6 Dr. Howard A. Rusk (1901-1989) became the first chairman of New York University's new department of physical medicine and rehabilitation in 1946. In 1951 he opened the Institute that would later be named after

him. Active in military medicine during and after the Korean War, he envisioned comprehensively rehabilitating the whole war-torn country. He believed that ninety percent of severely disabled people could be taught to hold a job and "work with dignity." He was passionate about the rights of the disabled to contribute to society and thereby contribute to the well-being of the entire nation.

So it came about that Glenn could start putting his life together again. Although he would graduate six months behind his original class (1954), it signified little to him. Having spent three months in the Los Angeles Rehabilitation Center of Rancho Los Amigos, he moved east for his internship. A year later, he took his residency at the Institute at Bellevue, mentored by Dr. Howard Rusk himself (1956-1958).[7] Indeed, this top-flight treatment center had opened just five years before Glenn's arrival.

Young Glenn had already been described as a "living example of what a handicapped person can do." Yes, like other intelligent young physicians, he was hardworking and compassionate. He also liked a good joke. (He would learn to pilot a plane, sail a boat, and go river rafting too.)[8]

When Dr. Glenn Reynolds phoned Tim Greaves in New York, the conversation was truly a tonic for the patient. "Don't give up. You'll like what they do there at the institute." The spirited wheelchair doctor urged grass-roots courage. " Fight back for life. I had to, after polio got me."

Tim listened.

Once arrived in New York he came under the direct supervision of Dr. Rusk. To be sure, Tim Greaves' case was far more complicated than that of a polio patient. Still, as Dr. Rusk always liked to say, "I am an incurable optimist."

To the average man on the street, however, the word "rehabilitation" implies that a person might get back to where he or she started. In the same way, a "convalescent home" suggests that patients recover and go home. Both cases may be a dead end.

Nonetheless, Tim reached New York equipped with a fighting spirit. He had little else left. Ahead of him lay ten months of grueling effort to learn to cope with his physical and emotional circumstances.

From time to time, the exercises became very painful. Sometimes his progress seemed almost infinitesimal. The temptation to give up and drop

In 1973, Bellevue Hospital built the very contemporary building above, which became known as "The Cube"—a striking contrast to the original hospital, which 275 years ago started out as an almshouse.

out never ceased to stalk the halls of the institute. "I saw seventeen-year-old kids lapse into terrible depressions. Some of their relatives were unsympathetic," Tim recalled. "Other kids just couldn't relate to their condition. They became hateful and refused to cooperate with the hospital staff."

In his first weeks at Bellevue, Tim simply saved his strength for essentials. He felt too weak to follow the promptings of his restless mind. "But," he promised himself, "I refuse to lie here and become a vegetable."

One of his first visitors was Gordon, a medical student from New York University's School of Medicine. "Hey, man! You're in my bed!"

"Your bed?" Tim looked at him in astonishment.

"Yes, I was in that bed for three months." Gordon whacked the footboard. "A spinal tumor. Had to learn to walk all over again."

Tim watched as Gordon, with agility,

---

7 Upon completing his residency in Rehabilitation Medicine, Glenn Reynolds worked at the Washington Adventist Hospital, Takoma Park, Maryland, for the next fifteen years.
8 Gail McBride, "Glenn Reynolds MD: A Matter of Attitude" *JAMA.* 1981:245(21) 2149-2151.

Tim prized his ability (after the stage had been set) to feed himself. He thoroughly enjoyed dining out with his friends.

stepped to a bedside chair. He sat down and deftly crossed his legs. "Two med students in a row," he mused. "What a coincidence! They must be out to get us."

Tim found his visitor exciting, of course, and positive. He realized that he would never be able to do what Gordon was doing. He determined, however, to push himself as far as he could go.

Then Gordon voiced the question that had been edging around in Tim's mind for months. "Are you going back to med school when you get out of here?"

Tim had been thinking about it, of course. No one could really guess how much. "Well, I'd like to, but … I don't know. I don't think Loma Linda University ever had a case just like mine. They might not want me."

"Not want you?" The irrepressible Gordon clapped his hands on the arms of his chair with decision. "Well, then, just stay here and finish up at NYU. They'd take you. They made a place for me."

"Well, thank you, Gordon, but I'll try my own school first. You know. Back to California." Tim heard himself say this with surprising confidence. Gordon's optimism proved to be infectious.

Inside, however, Tim felt otherwise. What

kind of a doctor could he be now? He'd gone just far enough to know that he deeply loved the medical profession. Loved it intensely.

Occasionally, his mind wandered back to his childhood love of history. Maybe a history teacher could get along with just a functioning head. (If he had a good one!) Or maybe he could go into speech pathology. Nonetheless, he always came back to base one. Somehow, some way, he would have to go on in medicine. He knew that he had to be altogether devoted to that career.

Finally, the day came when he could go down to the hospital library and read. Tim's choice of books now took a predictable turn. He read *It's Good to Be Alive* by Roy Campanella, longtime catcher for the old Brooklyn Dodgers. Of necessity, as a resident of the United States, Tim had transferred his early love of cricket to baseball. Wherever. Whenever. Tim had a passion for sports. Because Campanella had suffered an injury identical to Tim's in a freak automobile accident, his disability and life story spoke powerfully to the woebegone young medical student.

Eventually, each day at the center began to bring its own little victory, especially after his right arm was fitted with a brace. No power returned to the hand, but he achieved some movement in his right shoulder and a little in his wrist. The break had not been quite horizontal, and that left a little movement from the shoulder. It seemed then a pitifully small boon, but it gave Tim just the morsel of freedom that his vigorous, inventive spirit craved.

The ability to manipulate his right thumb and two fingers opened up a whole new world of mobility. "I can spend hours alone," Tim said years later. He propelled his electric wheelchair in and out of his office, up and down the halls, and onto the elevators. Only when he reached his car in the parking lot did he have to rely on his attendant to transfer him from the chair and into the seat.

"I remember so well the day I began feeding myself. It was such a marvelous thing!" The pleasure at such independence brought him near tears. The marvel of holding an apple and biting into its tart sweetness all by himself! A heady moment, indeed. "I can remember how it tasted between my teeth!"

Along with these daily victories, Tim worked through the slow, steady demands of emotional adjustment. In learning to accept himself as he was, he could look ahead calmly to life as he would have to live it. Thus, the old appetite for life slowly began to return.

Immediately after the accident, physicians had put Tim on low doses of what they called a "psychic energizer." Naturally, everyone expected him to fall into deep depression. To be sure, he had reason enough! Although he could not know how things might have been without the drug, Tim concluded that it offered only minimal help. When the doctors took him off it six months later, he had no withdrawal symptoms. He attributed his relative freedom from depression to a much Higher Source than drugs.

Bad days, of course, did come. He remembered his twenty-fifth birthday as a particularly gloomy time, perhaps one of the worst days of all. The debris of broken plans and shattered hopes threatened to overwhelm him as he lay in his bed at the rehab center. What am I now? Where am I? And why am I?

The old questions drummed through his mind until he felt that his body prison would crush him. "Yes," he recalled, "I was weeping. Then a nurse came in with medications and found me there."

He cared nothing then about trying to be "manly." It was one of those fragile, fleeting little male-female encounters. "She patted my head. Then she kissed her hand and laid her cool fingers on my lips." She said nothing. Just that, and then she walked out of the door. "But it helped somehow," Tim mused. "It helped."

His various visitors brought with them their own individually tailored kinds of comfort and counsel. One minister he had long admired offered him Psalm 20:7: "Some trust in chariots, some in horses, but we will remember the name of the Lord our God." Yes, Tim could no longer run with the horses and chariots. He couldn't even keep up with the footmen. "But I knew I could

stand on the name of the Lord our God."

One special-duty nurse read Psalm 27:14: "Wait on the Lord: be of good courage, and he shall strengthen thine heart." Tim would learn to wait. He would learn almost infinite patience.

Of necessity, the patterns of Tim's spiritual life changed. "I can remember, as we all do, praying in panic," he said. By now, his valley had been too long and too dark for him to find support in mere panic praying. He developed an entirely different perspective on devotions.

At first, he drew only on what he had previously assimilated into his Christian life. "Sometimes I felt very alone and leaned heavily upon my spiritual resources." But he could no longer kneel for the more "programmed" type of prayer. He could not reach for a book to read a comforting passage. "Lying there on my back, I began to have a kind of ongoing communication with God. Scriptures would come to mind just when I needed them."

In his devotional reading, nothing appealed to Tim more than the Biblical book of Job. When tempted—daily—to cry out, "Why? Why did this happen to me?" Tim discovered new and poignant meanings he'd never dreamed possible before in the ancient Hebrew drama. The thousands of years in time and thousands of miles in distance seemed as nothing. The young patient in the wheelchair in New York understood, as few others could, the plight of the stricken man on the ash heap back in the Land of Uz. These understandings formed the foundation of the philosophy of suffering that Tim was to build on for the rest of his life.

As each hospital night stretched on into an equally long hospital day, and as the night-morning-night cycle rolled on interminably, another scripture took on a new glory. It made each day livable. "It is of the Lord's mercies that we are not consumed, because his compassions fail not. They are new every morning: Great is Thy faithfulness" (Lamentations 3:22, 23). For Tim, each morning held a peculiar kind of challenge. Every day he had to accomplish a "rebirth" for himself.

Mornings brought blessings also. Tim remembered, again, the firm, sure voice of his dear old grandmother, Christian Boyce, in Barbados, singing her favorite worship song:

> *New mercies, each returning day,*
> *Hover around us while we pray;*
> *New perils past, new sins forgiven,*
> *New thoughts of God, new hopes of heaven.*

Above and over all stood his parents, Eric and Evelyn Greaves. He believed that, without them and the sacrifices they made, he could never have survived. Probably he was right.

Dr. Claran Jesse had phoned the Eric Greaves family in Trinidad on that bleak May day in 1959 to tell them of the accident. When Mom Evelyn caught the solemn tenor of his voice, she thrust the telephone receiver into her husband's hands. "It … it … it must be about Tim," she quavered.

From that moment forward, the family support system leaped into service. A frantic series of events took place as the family accommodated to the tragedy. Long, long years of recuperation lay ahead. Eric and Evelyn arrived in California ten

days after the accident. His mother's first trip to America, however, had none of the thrills of tourism. Instead, everything centered on the still form of her son she found lying on the hospital bed.

Tim spoke of this emotional reinforcement in awe. "Such complete and perfect family support. Just like the God they had taught me to trust." His mother stood by him, while his father gave her the love and home security that made the long months of their future separation possible. As soon as Tim arrived at the rehab center in New York, they both flew in again from Trinidad to be there and visit him every day. "I know how very, very fortunate I have been."

In the long months ahead, this thread of optimism would certainly not be wasted. On the other hand, it probably made acceptance harder. "I was determined that if I had to have a wheelchair, it would at least be a manual one. I would operate it under my own power.

"Of course, in the end I had to bury my pride." Tim would smile ruefully down at the streamlined motorized chair in which he spent his days. "I guess that's what it was. I had to give in to an electric wheelchair." In a perfectly rational way, he realized that submission was the only practical thing to do.

"So, one by one, I grew to accept some of the limitations. At least I did mentally. Still, I suppose, my initial reaction was disbelief. I just could not think that the injury could be as severe as it turned out to be."

A sudden crisis in anyone's life calls forth one inevitable question: "Why me? Lord, why me?" The unsaid (but heavily implied) part of the same question is "Why not someone else?" When people like Tim come through victoriously, however, one finds that they have—perhaps even unconsciously—rephrased the question. They have inquired, sincerely, "Why not me, Lord?"

"Job's Complaint" by William Blake (1757-1827).[9] **Not surprisingly, Tim Greaves took refuge and much comfort in the promises of the Book of Job.**

9 The London poet and artist, William Blake, addressed the perennial question: "Why do good people suffer?" His twenty-two "Illustrations of the Book of Job" are masterpieces of his engraving skills.

At the same time, Tim had to work through a long sequence of thought. His initial reaction to his disaster was, "What did I do wrong? What am I being punished for?" He even recalled having taken Communion just two weeks earlier. "Did I partake unworthily?" he wondered.

Friends stepped in to talk Tim toward sanity and acceptance. He shared his anxieties with his classmate, Lindbergh Gallimore. "Look, man, God didn't do this to you," Lindy exclaimed. "That's not fair to Him." The ensuing conversation pushed Tim out of his lapse into legalism, revamped his outlook, and eased his guilt.

In time, Tim could laugh as he recalled folksy fragments of his Caribbean childhood. "The Guyanese have a saying, 'Don't take on worry.'" So he quickly decided not to take on this worry and vowed never to pursue the question of "Why me?"

When he arrived in New York, he knew he was right. "I saw people there who had utterly destroyed themselves in bitterness. I never wanted to get vengeful and hostile like that. Also, I knew that I had an enormous advantage over so many of my fellow patients—a powerful support system."

Even though he had love and support, his road remained a rocky one. One of his college faculty acquaintances, apparently unaware of the extent of Tim's injury, jovially declared, "You're young. You have great recuperative powers." But there are some things that even a young body cannot do. Tim knew that his spirit had to recuperate to make up for the failure of his body to do so. That was his reality.

By midlife, Tim Greaves had come to a very mature conclusion about himself. "I have to see my accident as an event in the interplay of good and evil. Just a little part of the great life puzzle. I accept it as such. I could wish it otherwise, of course, but I do accept it." His cheerful freedom from self-pity and bitterness was always very refreshing. He simply accepted himself as he was. In mathematical terms, perhaps, the axiom would read: "People accept you insofar as you accept yourself."

Doubtless, this was one of Tim's great success secrets. Indeed, one used to be able to visit with Tim and entirely forget that he was handicapped. Then he would make some awkward little movement that served as a reminder of his condition. The realization, however, often came as a surprise. One really had forgotten!

Intensive suffering has paradoxical results. A person may become self-righteous and introverted. Or vindictive—"I had to go through this trial, and I want you to do it too." He/she may even become indifferent to the pain of other people. In contrast, Tim took the high road. Although he became even more assertive than he had been before, he allowed the spirit and the grace of God to shape his character. A daily submission that he made virtually to the last day of his life.

Thus, by these means, Tim established a strong, personal identity. He did become somebody. That, indeed, was true by any measurement one might wish to apply.

Tim Greaves never missed a joke, and he dearly loved to laugh—one of his many marks of maturity.

Chapter 5

Crashing the Gates

Meanwhile Tim's doctors and professors back in Loma Linda, California, monitored his progress. Of the many Westerners traveling to the East, an amazing number of them seemed to find time to stop off at the Rehabilitation Institute and visit Tim during the ten months he spent in New York.

The idea of Tim's return to medical school met with mixed reactions on all sides. Naturally, the central question was: "Is he able to continue in medical school?" Some of the CME administrators thought not, and more than one visitor came to the institute to try to dissuade Tim. Although he didn't want to be unrealistic in his ambitions, Tim prayed for the chance to try. Just one chance.

One day, he met Dr. Howard Rusk in the hallway. "How does it go, Tim?" the institute director inquired casually.

"I'm not sure. Perhaps I should just give up and go home to Trinidad." Tim's eyes wandered over the dreary green hospital walls. "But somehow I can't give up the idea of a career in medicine. I know there must be some things I can do."

Immediately at attention, the compassionate doctor looked down at him, reading him through and through, it seemed. He'd seen more dramatic comebacks than anyone in an ordinary medical school could ever have hoped to see. "OK then, Tim. Let me handle this."

Dr. Rusk wrote to the College of Medical Evangelists and promised to help Tim get an internship when he finished. The process turned out to be complicated. Some of the faculty thought it could be done. Others viewed the venture as impossible. The school had never dealt with a quadriplegic student before. Paraplegic, yes. (They all could remember Glenn Reynolds.) But a quad? For one thing, how could he even perform a basic patient examination?

In later years, Dean Gordon Hadley remarked, "Tim Greaves was the first quadriplegic physician we had to deal with. Members of the administration were torn between compassion for our student, and the physical difficulties everyone had to face. Indeed," Dr. Hadley added, "Greaves was the first quadriplegic physician to graduate in the whole of the United States."

So Tim waited. Finally, Loma Linda was persuaded. He re-entered on a provisional basis to complete his second year of medicine. Actually he spent almost a year just readjusting to campus life. With such enormous handicaps, he utterly

Rehabilitation completed, Tim and his parents boarded a flight in New York to return to California (1960).

Left. At first Tim had a kind of homemade, fragile tilt frame in which to stand. Right. At his graduation his initial classmates (CME class of 1961) gave him a state-of-the-art tilt frame that provided him with daily "exercise." Later, surrounded by laughing friends, Tim covered his face in an uncommon gesture of shyness.

determined to "do it right."

With the help of parents, teachers, and classmates, Tim now began to get control of his life again. He rented a little apartment on Prospect Street within easy distance of the school buildings. Small as it was, it accommodated the many people who came and went, ministering to Tim's needs.

First, he had to study for his board examinations in pharmacology and pathology. Once that was done, Dr. Harold Shryock hired Tim as a reader for the anatomy lab that he taught for dental students.

Moreover, the good doctor would come and pick up Tim and then take him home. Bit by bit, Dr. Shryock drew his student back into the academic circle. Also, Tim tasted the independence of a little income and the responsibility of some work that lay within the range of his abilities. Tim always credited Dr. Shryock's interest and shaping influence as a pivotal force in his rehabilitation process. The professor himself built a ramp so that he could wheel Tim into the anatomy lab.

In the two years it took Tim to complete medical school, he not only learned some amazing lessons about himself but also about the unique school he attended. In the early years, the College of Medical Evangelists suffered from a certain academic prejudice. Even after Tim graduated in 1963, more than one journalist described his *alma mater* derogatorily as simply a "one-star medical school."

That kind of infamy lasted for at least fifty years. However, based on his own experience, Tim always gave Loma Linda a full five stars. It might also be added that Tim's own performance during his time there should be fixed in at the same level!

Tim also benefited from one of the things that Loma Linda has always done so well—the enduring excellence of relationships among classmates. Tim's group outdid themselves.

Arguably, a special bonding of friends occurs most securely in challenging—sometimes dangerous—situations. It happens among the police, firefighters, and in the military services. The shared discipline of medical school must also be included in this classification. People facing the greatest challenges can enter into the most intense kind of companionship. In contrast, occupations given over to moneymaking, legal, or political affairs often scatter emotions. They are as likely to create enemies as comrades.

The caregivers came and went. For his last two years of medical school, Tim and his mother lived in a duplex near the Los Angeles campus of the University, White Memorial Hospital.

Faithful friends like Lloyd Stoll (his former roommate) and Milford Thomas never begrudged the extra time it took to come by and help Tim out of bed and into his wheelchair. His friends cheerfully took turns wheeling him to class. In labs, when there was something important to see, no one maneuvered Tim's chair into the foreground more effectively than Lindy Gallimore. Tim never lacked for an energetic friend to help him to the optimum position up front.

All the same, his position remained a little tenuous for several months. It was hard to know exactly how things would turn out. "A field trip to Kaiser Steel Mills in Fontana was the Lord's providence," Tim recalled. During the tour, Dr. Frank Lemon, associate professor of public health (who worked there), spotted Lindy. He drew him aside. "Tell me. How's Tim doing?"

"Actually, he's doing very well. We're all helping him." Then Lindy leaned forward conspiratorially. "But he really needs someone to take his case in hand."

Dr. Lemon got the message. As "faculty champion," he set to evaluating credits and searching for precedents. Dr. Rusk from Bellevue advised and offered helpful suggestions. Thus, Tim's case became a cause that involved many people.

For one thing there had to be money. There were the good ladies from the nearby Community Services Center. Also many others who could not be so easily identified. Tim actually never knew where all of the letters came from. Funding came from the government, and tuition came from other sources.

Particularly, he remembered Justine Smadbeck, who administered the Jesse Smith-Noyes Foundation Fund for black students in medical schools. Just before the car crash, Tim had applied for and received this subsidy. Now, Justine heroically stood by, a true friend. (She even visited Tim in New York.) She carried Tim through the paperwork and far beyond. By the time he got back into medical school, a monthly stipend ($50) had kicked in. Finally, he was assigned a social worker. To his last day, Tim had to acknowledge that he, more than anyone else, "owed so much to so many."

None of these external grants, however, equaled his parents' support. His father, Pastor Eric Greaves, left his post as the chief administrative officer for the Seventh-day Adventist Church in the Eastern Caribbean. "Truly, my father sacrificed his own career for mine," Tim declared.

On graduation day, Dr. Timothy S. Greaves was wheeled up the ramp at the Redlands Bowl to receive his degree. A storm of applause broke out, followed by a standing ovation. Neither he nor anyone else who was in the Bowl on June 2, 1963, would ever forget that day.

The event confirmed two achievements for Tim. First, he felt the usual heady sense of accomplishment that he shared with his classmates. After all, becoming a physician is never really an ordinary event. Second, and much more importantly, he had adequately proved to himself that he could keep up with his profession, physical besetments notwithstanding.

That same year of Tim's graduation, his parents celebrated their thirtieth wedding anniversary. The whole family, including Tim, and many relatives converged on the Cave Hill Church, back home in Barbados. This trip set the pace for a great deal of travel yet to come. Tim simply would not allow his wheelchair to get in the way of what he wanted to do and where he wanted to go.

Of course, the demands of internship and residency still lay ahead. Internal medicine would have been the choice of a totally "whole" Tim. Now, however, four possible fields lay open to him: dermatology, diagnostic radiology, psychiatry, and pathology. The "handicapped" Tim opted for the last. By this time, he had developed a real enjoyment in the complex world of microscopic investigation.

Subsequently, he entered Loma Linda's four-year pathology residency. He would still work comfortably with the same good, supportive people with whom he had become so familiar by now. "Once accepted into the residency, I was treated just like anyone else." Tim made an important point of his new status. "That way, I could feel that I had really secured my place in the medical profession."

Within a few months, the Greaves family moved to Loma Linda where the University allotted them a little house on Mound Street. "Even though the rent was very low, we lived on a string for the next four years," Tim explained.

In this situation, the entire family carved out new lives for themselves. Although she was an astute, efficient graduate nurse, mother Evelyn worked the evening shift at a local nursing home. The supper-hour break gave her just enough time to run home and put Tim to bed. She took full care of her son during this time. Little sister Norma enrolled as a student at nearby La Sierra College (BA in library science and, later, MA in biology), and brother Donn attended Pacific Union College (pre-medicine). Father volunteered at a church in San Bernardino. Because he had many gifts, Eric Greaves silently made house repairs, resoled shoes, and, in general, kept the household afloat.[1]

Patient care, however, was not one of the pastor's strong points. Times when he was left alone with Tim, father and son had occasional head-on collisions. Both were glad when Mother came home. Invariably, Evelyn Greaves had the "touch" they both needed.

Tim, however, recalled those years as "good ones." United, the family carried one another past first one milestone and then another. Behind them

Timothy Greaves surrounded by his staff in the Cytopathology Laboratory in Los Angeles County Hospital.

all stood an immeasurable store of physical endurance and emotional energy. "It was," Tim reflected, "a total family effort." Together they talked, planned, prayed, comforted, and salvaged Tim's career. "Mom stayed with me almost constantly for the first six years."

Under all circumstances, his father kept up his church work and made a home for the younger siblings. "Dad and my brother and sister made the sacrifice of having Mom away from home much of the time. Thousands of miles away, most of the time."

When Tim completed his four-year pathology residency, he faced a question that had been hovering in the background ever since the accident, seven years earlier. "Who, out there in the job market, will actually want me?"

The issue now moved sharply into the foreground. "Yes, I'd given it much thought. Even so, I think it bothered the people at Loma Linda University even more than it did me." Having produced this particular kind of pathologist, the administrators might well be asking themselves, "What is going to happen to Tim next?"

Meanwhile something very good had been at work for him. He had become particularly interested in cytopathology.[2] This happened during his

---

1 In the Caribbean Union of Seventh-day Adventists, Eric Greaves' accomplishments were noteworthy: Pastor, Evangelist, Publishing & Temperance Director, Conference President.

2 One of the many branches of pathology, cyto-pathology is the study of cells, their origin, formation, structure and function. Exfoliative Cytology is the microscopic examination of cells with samples taken from lesions,

Of Courage, Compassion, and Endurance

Living and practicing medicine in Los Angeles was never Tim Greaves' first career plan. His limitations, however, forced him to revert to plan B—that is, his mind focused on the medical needs of the Caribbean. To that end, he persuaded several of his friends and colleaves to think along the same lines—to go home and serve the islands. **Left.** Trinidad had had a succession of small clinics. One of the early ones was an old converted army barracks on Mucorapo Road, near Port-of-Spain. **Right.** A "dream team," led by Tim Greaves (far right), earnestly discusses the possibility of setting up specialty practices near the new Adventist Community Hospital in the capital of Trinidad. It was one of the most grievous disappointments of Tim's life when the project failed.

three-month rotation at Los Angeles County Hospital. There he became acquainted with Dr. C. P. Schwinn, director of the division of cytopathology. At that very convenient point in time, Dr. Schwinn had some postgraduate fellowships available. Tim received one of those prestigious awards.

His high-quality work duly noted, he was offered a full-time position at Los Angeles County Hospital-University of Southern California Medical Center. This opened the door to his pioneer work in cytology. In fact, in 1991, he flew to Columbus, Ohio, to write one of the first national examinations in that specialty. (Ultimately he became department chief of Exfoliative Cytology at LAC/USC.)

Tim's choice of pathology as a specialty was not entirely unexpected. It also had a curious little spin-off. From the start, he approached each new disease that he learned about from the same viewpoint. "Might I have that?" Not that he gave himself up to morbid hypochondria, but such an intense concern with detail appeared to be a feature of the very personal commitment that

secretions, and, sometimes by scraping or fine-needle aspiration.

marked all of his endeavors.

Now Tim officially transferred the operational skills he had learned in medical school to his laboratory. For example, he managed the telephone without help. When it rang, he knocked the receiver off the hook and dragged the cord toward him with braced thumb and forefinger. It took time, but his callers knew what the clatter on the line meant, and they waited.

Assistants around the Cytology Department spoke of him in a way that showed how highly they esteemed and admired him. He wore well. No one felt burdened by his presence—and that is a situation into which a handicapped person can easily slip and which everyone abhors.

On ordinary workdays Tim could be found on duty, studying the slides that his assistant had prepared for his inspection, stained in gaudy blues, browns, and reds. "This one is a well-advanced carcinoma," he might say, pointing to a particularly bizarre combination of colored tissue.

In Tim's presence, however, those slides somehow lost their coldly scientific qualities. Every one of them represented a living person out there. Someone whose life, hope, and happiness hung on the report that Dr. Greaves would send down. "We must learn to be personally detached from the trauma," Tim looked up from the slides. "Yet each one means a human life. A true doctor can never forget that."

Tim's job was to detect and diagnose malignancy, measure hormonal levels, and so forth. Yet, he never allowed clinical "sterility" to destroy his humanity. He had suffered too much to let that happen, ever.

Nonetheless, a great gulf still lies between life in the lab and life out of it, between the medical establishment and the patient. Tim functioned in a land of "high-octane" language. Obedient to the academic maxim, "publish or perish," his research appeared in at least ten scholarly journals.

A small sample from one abstract will show how far Tim's life could be removed from the labors of non-medical people:

> The presence of basaloid cells and ghost cells in FNA smears, associated with a cutaneous location of the lesion, was sufficient for a confident cytologic diagnosis of philmatrixoma. ... Prominent nucleoli in basaloid cells and smears containing refractile keratin clumps were also very useful clues.[3]

Lay people back away from this kind of writing. "There's something wrong here," we murmur nervously. "Can someone please fix it?"

Then we retire in anxious confusion, thankful that people like Tim are in there taking care of things for us.

Indeed, Tim felt perfectly at home in this universe. Both profession and place suited him. "I just liked the situation at Los Angeles County/USC," he concluded. "It felt right to me, so I stayed."

---

3 Quoted from the on-line article, "Pilomatixoma: Clincoipathologic Study of 51 Cases with Emphasis on Cytologic Features." On this project, Tim worked with five colleagues: Jun Wang (LLUMC), and four from pathology departments at UCLA and USC.

Chapter 6

A Journey to Love

Before his accident, Tim had taken all of the usual interests in girls. They consistently fell for his good looks and charismatic personality. Afterwards, the question of marriage took a unique place in his mind. He had always been fastidious about whom he dated. Although he survived his handicap with a measure of confidence, he viewed courtship with excessive caution. "Would you believe," Tim would marvel, "I've had more than one offer of marriage since I've been in the wheelchair!"

On the lighter side, he always had his office staff. "The girls like to kid around the lab here. They say they would be willing to help me spend my money." He studied his braced right arm quizzically. "Of course, no one takes that seriously."

Skillful as his many attendants had been, there remained a degree of trauma in changing companions so often. Many of his helpers were students from the West Indies, and Tim managed to make the benefits mutual. Still, the young people stayed on an average of only two years. (The longest was five.)

The frequent changes were hard on Tim. "I have missed the security of close, long-lasting relationships," Tim confessed. Shrugging his one shoulder ever so slightly in a gesture with his right arm, he added, "As yet I have not found anyone who wanted to spend the rest of life with me."

That is what Dr. Tim said in an early interview. When pressed on the matter, however, he would admit, "Of course, I would have to be very careful about finding the right one who could manage such a relationship." Then, with a knowing grin, he would admit, "But who knows! The thought is not entirely out of my mind."

Indeed, it was not.

Probably already he hoped—secretly—that Thelda would bring him the close, permanent re-lationship he craved. Right then, however, he kept that secret to himself.

Through the years of crises, ups and downs, and bafflement, the small person of Thelda Van Lange remained a vivid image from Tim's Trinidad high school days. Reserved and retiring, she loved and respected him. In fact, she waited. Waited for twenty-six years.

Thus, the journey began in Trinidad. Tim's father, Pastor Eric Greaves, had been caring for five churches at once, including the Curepe Church, which Thelda attended with her family. One night at Pastor Greaves' evangelistic crusade in Barataria, Thelda found herself singing in a ladies' octet from her church. Throughout the song, "A Little Talk with Jesus Makes It Right," Tim never took his eyes off her. He later admitted that "something happened" to him that evening.

Thelda, on the other hand, had no inkling of what was transpiring right in front of her. Only later did she discover the variety of family connections that already existed between Tim and her.[1] "Yet he was never one to openly 'talk his heart.' So I just kept wondering if that powerful upperclassman would ever really notice me."

Over the long years, correspondence linked Tim and Thelda together. Reserved as they were, on both sides, the letters came steadily. Using CME letterhead, Tim, at first, wrote with an even hand—better than one might expect from a would-be physician.

One afternoon after school Thelda and some friends waited at the bus stop by the college. Tim pulled up in his father's car. "May I give you a ride home?" he inquired gallantly.

This was the first time that he had ad-

---

1 Thelda's aunt, Marjorie Van Lange, had married Vasco Boyce who was Tim's cousin and also a close friend of Thelda's cousins, Lloyd and Kennard Stoll. Her young Uncle Ivan Van Lange was a friend of Tim's. The school, Caribbean Training College, had drawn all of these young people together.

Left. Thelda stood between her cousins, Beulah and Vernon Andrews. She was a very little girl when she went to Trinidad to live with her Uncle Sim and Aunt Winifred. Right. The S. C. Andrews home on Wellington Steet, St. Joseph, Trinidad, where Thelda grew up.

dressed her personally, and every fiber in her being told her to hold back. " But—but—what about my friends?" Instinctively, she wanted to defend herself.

"Oh, they can come too," Tim replied casually. "But I want you to sit in the front seat beside me."

As usual, Tim's seriousness intimidated her, making him the adult and her the youngster. "That night, he asked me what I wanted to do when I 'grew up.'" She felt very small. Would he ever really pay attention to her? Who could tell?

"I have always wanted to be a nurse," she replied. That answer seemed to satisfy him.

From childhood, Thelda could remember her mother saying, "When you grow up, my girl, you'll be a nurse." Indeed, a kind of predestination had begun to work in her young life.

In the home of her Uncle Sim Andrews in Trinidad, Thelda had to excel. He determined that she and her two cousins would learn. He would never allow them be slackers. He reminded them that when he took his first telegraphy examinations, he was "first on our island topping his class." On Sundays, after morning worship, he would instruct the children in history, poetry, arithmetic, and spelling.

Above all, he deplored the mispronunciation of words. With missionary zeal he sought to rescue them from the natural linguistic idiosyncracies of the Caribbean. "You do not say 'Dis.' The word is 'This,'" he lectured. "And I want to hear 'that,' not 'dat.'" Uncle Sim tolerated none of this kind of slovenly speech around his house. No one was exempt.

From time to time, he would take the three youngsters on outings. While they enjoyed these excursions well enough, they knew what had to come next. Upon returning home, her uncle required each one of them to write an essay about their adventure. No matter what they wrote, it was never quite good enough for Uncle Sim. With such persistent conditioning, Thelda had no trouble passing English in her Senior Cambridge Exams (1956). She had plenty of training in writing essays.

By this time Tim had gone north to Emmanuel Missionary College (now Andrews

Thelda Van Lange taught at the Government School for Girls in Port-of-Spain, Trinidad (1965).

University), in Michigan. Now he and Thelda exchanged letters. Not frequent but dependably regular. One summer, Tim had a memorable book-selling adventure.

In Evansville, Indiana, he rapped on a door and gave his usual canvass to the woman. "She paid little attention to the book," he recalled. "Instead she made an offer. 'I'll buy the book if you kiss me.'"

"No! I won't do that," he snapped, stepping back in astonishment.

"Well then, I suppose you have a girlfriend," the would-be client went on. "Do you?"

"Yes, I do." Tim heard himself say it in a very loud voice. The picture of Thelda Van Lange popped into his head. True, he had not yet mentioned any such arrangement to that lovely girl back in Trinidad. No matter. He knew that the thought had sprung from a very deep place in his heart.

A few days later, the woman showed up at his door to renew her quest. In a way, his masculine pride might have been slightly aroused.

Mainly, however, he was frightened. How in the world had she found where he lived? In any case, he knew that he was committed to a higher quality of friendship than anything she had to offer.

Tim had been brought up in a strictly moral household, so his resistance didn't surprise Thelda. Given her own background and personality, she had long ago decided that she was not going to live through a long series of little flirtations.

Who has not contemplated "tragedy" as teenagers stagger from one heartbreak to the next? "I didn't want to live in a constant state of anguish. I just wanted to find The One and stop there," Thelda declares.

Ultimately, she was to discover that Tim, despite his profound maturity, had broken several hearts with "little loves" along the way. Still, she regarded the account of his Indiana episode calmly enough. It spoke well of his standards. Besides, her heart had not been shattered. He had given her no reason yet to persuade her to make any kind of emotional investment.

Moreover, Thelda had far too many practical things to think about. She alone had to find a way to pay for her own education. So, she taught in a local elementary school. Although she vacationed at home in Guyana whenever she could, she frugally saved money for her next step in education. Like Jacob wooing Rachel, it took seven years for her to reach her goal.

Meanwhile, Tim had arrived in medical school at Loma Linda. He continued writing to Thelda at widely spaced, though fairly regular, intervals.

Although Thelda never talked much about her feelings, she dutifully showed the first letter to her Aunt Winifred. In a family that didn't share a lot of open communication, little was said of the matter.

Tim wisely avoided what Thelda describes as "love stuff." He felt (rightly) that Thelda's watchful Uncle and Aunt Andrews might not approve of him. In fact, long years would pass before Tim could learn how to cope with the possibility of rejection. He had to balance himself between his natural leadership traits and this instinctive tendency to fear.

One Christmas, he sent Thelda a presumably "safe" Christmas gift, the current morning devotional book. Greatly disturbed, Uncle Sim insisted that she return it. Tim had not asked formally to be allowed to write to Thelda, and this omission surely had to mean instability! The "old school" from which the Andrews came believed that if a young man asked for "parental permission" to correspond, he must be serious—that is, less likely to jilt the girl. Centano Andrews was trying to be a responsible uncle and protect his niece from disappointment.

Thelda, however, stood her ground. Firstly, she didn't want to offend Tim. Secondly, no one had any cash to spare, so why should all of that money (the book and the postage) be wasted. She got her way.

Meanwhile, one girl had been writing to Tim every week. "I just don't have time for this," he finally told her. No doubt an element of truth existed in that statement, given the labors of medical students. At the same time, he informed Thelda: "I have told my mother that I am writing to you."

So correspondence between Loma Linda and Trinidad continued. Not at a panic pace but steadily.

Then came that terrible Sunday morning. Thelda was home in St. Joseph. Fifteen-year-old Joel Jones entered the house for piano lessons from her cousin, Vernon Andrews. "Did you hear about Tim Greaves?" the lad exclaimed. "He was in a bad accident. He may not live." The room froze in time and space. "The doctors say he could live only three months!" The very air congealed in fear.

Slowly the narrative evolved among the family. Instinctively, everyone could recall Tim leaping up the stairs two at a time. They could hear his deep voice telling everyone exactly what he expected them to do next. Yes, he had been anointed. He had been prayed over. Suddenly, people all through the lower Caribbean islands were pleading for a miracle of healing. But the healing didn't happen. Instead, the

Letters from Tim to Thelda. Top. Before. Bottom. After.

Thelda Van Lange had a large farewell at the eight-grade school the day she left to begin her nurses' training in Michigan (1965).

laws of nature prevailed. A broken neck like Tim's resulted in total paralysis.

In the first days following the shocking news Thelda, like everyone else, froze into utter disbelief. She visited his parents, Eric and Evelyn Greaves. Everyone tried desperately to believe and hope for the best, whatever that was going to be.

After the initial uproar, Thelda withdrew to quiet, private thoughts. Although she said little, her mind was constantly centered on Tim. Would he really die or live?

During family worship one morning, she asked God for a sign. In one of those strange message transmissions that occasionally occur for Christians, she randomly opened her Bible. Her thumb rested on Psalm 118:17-18: "I shall not die, but I shall live, and recount the deeds of the Lord. The Lord has chastened me sorely, but he has not given me over to death."

Now Thelda could believe that Tim actually was going to live. She saw no possibility of marriage, of course. "I suppose I shall not marry anyone," she told herself. "I have always loved Tim, and it wouldn't be fair for any other husband to put up with that."

In his last letter to her before the crash, he casually remarked that he had been dating other girls. Why not? They had never had any kind of

agreement. Still, the terrible event deepened their relationship, although neither one of them seemed to realize it at the time.

Being forever a very private person, if the crippled Tim could not write himself, he could not bring himself to dictate his thoughts to another person. When he reached the Rehabilitation Center in New York, he learned how to use a typewriter. The first letter he picked out on the keyboard was to Thelda. Then he managed to write with a pen on a special "desk." The task was laborious and the writing nearly illegible. In any case, Tim had to try everything in his way.

Meanwhile, Thelda arrived in Michigan in mid-winter, 1965. Her seven years of saving money had ended. She enrolled at Andrews University and began her long-hoped-for pre-nursing program. At almost the same time, she began to develop a friendship with a young man attending another Christian college in the United States. Attractive and upstanding, he was a Christian gentleman and pursued his interest in Thelda in a very respectful way.

Finally, the time for decision came. Thelda had to work it out—just herself and God. Confiding in no one, she gave herself over to three days of fasting and prayer. What was Heaven's will and what would be the outcome with Tim? Like Gideon, she "put out her fleece" and awaited further instruction. "If I am to be with him, let me let me know Your will, Lord." She retreated to the tiny chapel in Lamson Hall and laid it all on Him.

She asked to receive a letter from Tim. (Quite a long silence had prevailed.) He would say one of two things. "There is no future in our relationship. You need to move on and find someone else." Or did he have another message of some kind? In either case, she prayed a letter from Tim would arrive.

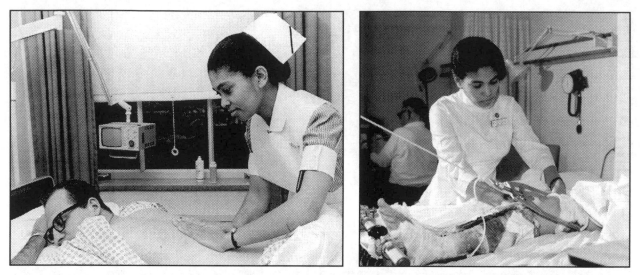

Left. Any patient at Hinsdale Adventist Hospital, in Illinois, would have gladly been attended by an efficient young lady like student nurse Thelda Van Lange. The custom of the starched apron and striped cap still prevailed, helping to make procedures aesthetically pleasing. Right. In the orthopedic unit at Loma Linda University Medical Center, Thelda examines the cast and traction equipment for an accident victim.

On the following Sunday afternoon when she returned from her job in College Wood Products, her roommate, Shirley Howell, met her at the door. "Look," her friend shouted, waving an envelope in her face. "You've got a letter from Tim!"

By this time, Thelda already had made important arrangements with God several times. Therefore, she wasn't exactly surprised. The contents of the letter, however, were surprising. Among other things, Tim spoke of how her letters and phone calls buoyed him up and gave him courage through his long months of hospitalization.

Thelda's request had been very specific. Now she had no option other than to tell her suitor that, after all, Tim—the tragically disabled Tim—was her true love. With his usual courtesy he gracefully stepped aside: "If I had known about your friendship with Norma Greaves' brother, I would never have interfered in any way."

This was not, by any means, the first romantic possibility that Thelda had allowed to lapse. Somehow, other potential friendships had always withered on the vine. Perhaps Tim had always been lurking in the back of her mind—maybe even way down at the subconscious level.

Although, for both Tim and Thelda, their professional careers were blossoming, romance somehow remained in the background. Always present but never really promoted.

For the year following her nursing diploma at Hinsdale Sanitarium and Hospital (1968) Thelda worked in the medical-surgical wards, with occasional assignments in orthopedics and the operating room. When she returned to Andrews University to finish her BSN degree (1971), her roommate, Marilyn Cathcart, went with her.

By this time, Tim had concluded his residency and a fellowship in cytopathology at Los Angeles County Hospital and University of Southern California. Now able to support a wife, he felt free to propose marriage that same year.

For some non-definable reason, Thelda heard herself saying no. True, she loved him and was sure that she could not marry anyone else. At the same time, she knew she wasn't ready. The commitment was enormous! Neither one of them, of course, could see down the road another ten years!

Silent months passed. There were still women aplenty wanting Tim's attention—wheelchair and all. Even a head nurse at Rancho Los Amigos Rehabilitation Center was very determined to

Of Courage, Compassion, and Endurance

marry him and earnestly set herself to the task! Everything in his private life, however, seemed to have gone dark, and he fell into deep depression. He was by no means accustomed to having his plans fall through.

The next year, Thelda and Marilyn (Cathcart) moved to Loma Linda. Marilyn received a scholarship and started classes. Several work opportunities opened to Thelda. Although it was not her first choice, she accepted an appointment in the orthopedics department. Over the next ten years, she would learn how to care for severely injured patients, including quadriplegics.

Upon arrival in California, Thelda received a call from Norma Greaves, Tim's sister. "I think you should call Tim." She went on to report that she heard someone asking her brother about Thelda. "He looked so unhappy. He said he knew nothing about you—not even where you are."

A regretful Thelda hung up the phone and considered the matter. Really, she had no reason not to talk to him. She did call, and found a perfectly receptive Tim on the other end of the line. No scolding.

Immediately, the courtship was on again.

Still, both remained very wary. When they met at home gatherings and meetings, however, the encounters were always pleasant. After all,

Thelda had said no, and she could not be sure that Tim was not still intimidated by the whole prospect of marriage.

In 1978, in reaction to the destruction of Tim's first "Trinidad Dream," he tried to allay his disappointment by asking for a sabbatical year from USC. At the time, his brother Donn was setting up his practice in obstetrics and gynecology in Bridgetown, Barbados. Donn saw to it that Tim lived a life as full and rewarding as the one he had built for himself in Los Angeles.

Tim taught in the Faculty of Medicine at the University of the West Indies and consulted at the Queen Elizabeth Hospital department of pathology in the Medical Center. Given his strong work ethic and professionalism, the university asked him to stay. Becoming reacquainted with his homeland, he found the proposition very tempting.

Tim would later remember this year as the highlight of his career. There, too, he had leisure to enjoy the old Greaves' home overlooking the ocean at Cave Hill. Indeed, Tim would gladly have remained in Barbados. The practical necessities of his daily life, however, were simply too difficult. He had to reach the rational decision: "Go back to where you came from."

While Tim was gone, Thelda completed her master's degree in public health. She also discov-

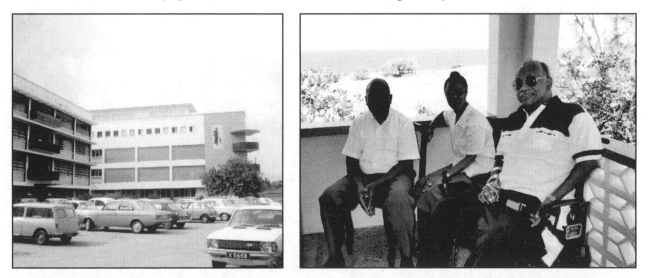

Left. Queen Elizabeth Hospital, Barbados. Right. The Greaves' family home at Cave Hill, Barbados. Tim relished every opportunity to be home and to become better acquainted with his many relatives on the island.

ered that she truly missed him. Did this really translate into love? Still, two things kept delaying progress. Thelda would not push herself forward. She was waiting to be assured that Tim still loved her, and that going forward was still God's plan.

On the other hand, the very strength that enabled Tim to survive also made it difficult for him to "talk romance." She wondered. Possibly he now felt so secure in himself that he didn't need her. Nonetheless, by the time he got back to California, Thelda decided that, if Tim proposed again, she would say yes this time.

One Sunday, his ever-faithful attendant, Webster Brown, brought Tim out to Grand Terrace for another visit. The tenor of the conversation became intimate. Thinking to try a new approach, Thelda mustered enough courage to inquire, "Tim, are you asking me to marry you?"

"No." The self-possessed wheelchair doctor appeared to know his own mind. She retreated. She could wait. After all, it had already been 26 years. If the whole process had not been so important, the entire matter might have been laughable. In later years, in fact, they did comprehend the humor of this stage of their love affair.

What happened next appeared, in hindsight, to be simply a leveling of the playing field, as it were. She had said no to him once. He had said no to her once. Perhaps this insight reveals a little perversity in the male mind. And hers too, for that matter. In any case, the situation worked in Tim's brain and soothed his innate fear of failure.

To be sure, women being attracted to a wheelchair doctor gave a man certain ego satisfaction. When all was said and done, however, he felt his truly strong confidence only with Thelda. They had known one another from childhood. In actual fact, there never had really been anyone else for either one of them.

Quite suddenly, the romantic drama moved into its last act. Dr. Timothy Greaves proposed to Nurse Thelda Van Lange, and she accepted. They set the date for June 28, 1981. Over her years of nursing experience, Thelda had learned that quadriplegic marriages were not only possible, but that they could last too.

The wedding was late by more than an hour when an elderly relative became ill. In the interim, Tim philosophically resigned himself to the long delay. By nature, he tolerated such delays with difficulty. On this his wedding day, he patiently waited out the time.

Even at this point, however, many things seemed tentative. Truly, it was colossal commitment. Poor Thelda kept asking God that, if it was an unwise decision, He would throw a barrier in the way. Instead, plans went forward without a hitch.

When her nursing supervisor, Elsie McLellan, and the staff heard the news, they threw themselves into the task with a will. All together, they beautifully coordinated the entire wedding. It seemed that everyone in Loma Linda knew Tim. They uniformly approved the match. "Oh, he's a neat guy." In effect, every possible cause for doubt had finally been snatched out of Thelda's hands.

Even on that memorable day, as Donn was getting Tim put together for the ceremony, he asked, "Well, boy, do you know what you're doing?" Even that casual remark frightened the bridegroom. And the bride also had "nerves." Despite the many years they'd had to think about

**Dr. Timothy S. and Thelda Van Lange Greaves.
June 28, 1981, Loma Linda, California.**

it, the promises they made that day carried much more responsibility than wedding vows do for most people. For them, the "better or worse" part stood right beside them at the altar, almost like a living entity.

Tim sat in the arbor on the lawn, waiting, while his very lovely bride and her attendants zigzagged their way down the garden terrace path to join him. The engraved wedding invitation spoke of "the beginning of our life together." Those long-ago teenagers could never have foreseen the long, often inexplicably painful, path over which their friendship would travel.

One of the pieces of fine classical music featured in the service was Handel's "Where'er You Walk." Tim and Thelda received two particular gifts that day. First was Place. Together they would travel to a place where, as the musician Handel said, they walk in the cool shade of Heaven's eternal trees. Although Tim still had to travel in a wheelchair, they now could go forward, hand in hand.

Second, they received the gift of Time. Despite the decades of test and trial behind them, they would still have 29 years to spend together.

That unforgettable day brought tears to the eyes of more than one of the wedding guests.

The wedding party

Chapter 7

Housekeeping

Tim decided that, after so many years spent leading up to it, his and Thelda's honeymoon should be in a memorable place. In fact, in one of America's national historical landmarks, the Hotel del Coronado in San Diego, California.

Built in 1887, the magnificent complex was set in a barren island landscape given over to coyotes and sea gulls. With its colorful heritage, the huge Victorian seaside hotel grew into a living legend. When it opened with its 680 rooms and seven floors, it was the largest hotel in the world. Its guest list has been stunning, including eleven U.S. presidents along with European nobility. Also Aviator Charles Lindbergh (1920), Marilyn Monroe (1958), and other Hollywood types. When Prince Edward (VIII) banqueted at the Coronado in 1920, Wallis Simpson was living there at the time. (Did the ill-starred couple actually meet that night?)

None of these things particularly interested the bridal couple as they moved into this famous beach resort. (Probably not even the alleged resident ghost!) As two Caribbean islanders, it was simply enough that the salty Pacific Ocean breezes met them at the door of their suite. "We walked on the beach every day," Thelda remembers. Walked? Yes, well-placed sidewalks enabled Tim to "walk" without burying his wheelchair in the sand. Afterwards, fine dining at the restaurant.

Beyond all of this, other preparations had been made. For the occasion, Tim had bought a portable lift to get him in and out of the car. Who needed a third person—even a helpful attendant—on his honeymoon? By careful planning, Tim and Thelda had the freedom of being alone.

Over the years, Tim had worked out each of the moves that needed to be made to transfer him from one position to another. He himself gave

each attendant meticulous instructions on exactly how the job should be done.

After ten years as an orthopedic nurse, the bride felt that she had some skills but not nearly enough. "You can do it," Tim encouraged at each juncture.

It took Thelda almost two more years before she realized that she could actually manage Tim by herself. (Although she did so at the expense of her own health.) He patiently instructed, she obeyed, and it worked. The slip, the slide, the quick tug—she mastered them all, her small, dainty person notwithstanding. Then, the world opened up to them. Even when Thelda was not altogether sure that she could carry a proposed adventure to a successful end, the resourceful Tim invented ways to do it.

When Thelda and her Hinsdale nursing roommate, Marilyn, had completed their nurses' training, they moved to California. At the time, Tim and Thelda had been in a period of "romantic distance," and he did not even know that she was working in Loma Linda. The two girls spent two years in a house that they had purchased together in Redlands. Then they went on to buy their own houses.[1] Thelda then lived near her work in Loma Linda.

That little house was where the honeymooners spent the next week after they came home. Technically, it took her six months to complete her move to Tim's house in South Pasadena. They saw one another on weekends, while she completed her duties at Loma Linda University Medical Center and disposed of her house. The latter event benefited Thelda's family, immigrants from Guyana. First her father and her sister, followed

---

1 Marilyn Cathcart had gone to work as a nurse on a cruise ship, and their interests and times had separated.

shortly by her brother-in-law and a little flock of children, came to occupy the place.

Having never lost her first passion for nursing, Thelda worked for many years after her marriage. Her ultimate move to Pasadena, however, caused her to make a U-turn in her career. Two years at Glendale Hospital were followed by four years service as an occupational health nurse for Los Angeles County (1984-1988). Clinical testing for the police, firefighters, and all of the other county employees occupied her, day after day. Then came ten years in HIV epidemiology. Her investigations helped track the spread of AIDS in Los Angeles County.

Thelda retired in August, 2000. Not because she wanted to--she loved her work. Caring for Tim, however, evolved into an overwhelming schedule. Sending him off to work and then getting herself out the door to her own appointments became too difficult. Because she loved her husband much more than any kind of employment, she stopped. "I found myself so sleepy in the daytime." An embarrassed smile flickered across her face. "I knew what I had to do." Like Tim, she could never agree to anything other than 200 percent job performance.

From the first day he could manage to do it, Tim owned his own house! Having had such a vigorous personality before the accident made the emotional adjustments to his losses all the harder to take. So he took this material measure against overwhelming discouragement and self-pity. "I bought my own house and had it planned for the convenience of my wheelchair. It's a necessary refuge and gives me that certain independent dimension that I need."

Hotel del Coronado, San Diego, California

The entire household structure had to be operated as carefully as a guerilla camp. Because of rising gasoline prices, Tim frugally replaced his gas-guzzling Cadillac (purchased at an auction) with a little Honda Accord. The Honda held his folding wheelchair and lapboard but little else.

Fastidiously clean, Tim submitted each morning to a bed bath or a scouring in the tub. Anything else, if at all possible, he did for himself—combing his hair, brushing his teeth (hard) and shaving with his electric razor. Nothing docile or helpless about him. If he could do it: "Out of the way. Let me at it." If he couldn't: "Well then, get it done. Now."

Much of Tim's leisure life centered on the church. There he continually found good friends who "understand that I'm trying to be myself." Consider one of the Christmas banquets of West Indies College (now University of the Northern Caribbean) alumni. Observe the lively chatter of friends, the heavy-laden tables of a buffet dinner, and the mellow sounds of Trinidad's steel drums. There, in the middle of it all, one would find a smiling Tim. See that the lilting music is getting right into his bones. In fact, the table to which he wheels up his chair is likely to be one of the liveliest in the room.

By the time of his marriage, Tim had come a long way in the task of redeveloping his self-image. Professionally he was established. He had seniority as a civil servant in the Los Angeles County system. He also had hosts of friends.

Excellent taste, good grooming, and neat, color-coordinated clothes enhanced his lively personality. His professional appearance minimized the wheelchair to an amazing extent. "I always like to dilute the obviousness of my handicap as much as possible. For instance, when I go to a convention or other public place, I have my driver take me to a back door where he can transfer me to my wheelchair privately. Then I can arrive in public sitting tall and proper in my chair. It helps." At all times, Tim needed to feel "put together" and completely in charge.

Tim trained his office staff meticulously. When he arrived at work, they removed his backpack and retrieved his lunch box. (He always preferred home food to the hospital cafeteria.) Then, they attached his customized lap-tray/desk, and his workday began.

Tim once admitted, "I suppose my greatest difficulty has been finding attendants. I am dependent, of course, on others to exist." No doubt, that was one of the hardest circumstances he had to accept.

"I can't say that I've really had any rough experiences with my attendants." He twitched his right shoulder ever so slightly in a gesture with his right arm. "Oh, well, once some of my clothes and a TV got stolen. But then," he added mildly, "perhaps he needed them more than I did."

While his accident may have completely destroyed Tim's self-worth, it also threw him into an entirely new connection with people. Some friends came to visit him and some didn't. But Tim understood. "The reason they didn't come is

Thelda at work in Occupational Health, at the Hall of Administration in Los Angeles (1980s).

because they didn't know what to say. I don't look on it as rejection."

Indeed, Tim should have been diagnosed as an incurable "people person." From New York to Washington, Barbados to Trinidad, and back to Southern California—he always knew what was going on. Telephones linked him to the world.

His relationships with other people, of course, had been essential for his security, both physical and emotional. He reverted constantly to the "hard core" of friends who stood beside him before and after the accident. The wives of several of his classmates and teachers did many free eight-hour shifts of special-duty nursing. One girl worked sixteen-hour stints. (Eight hours of regular duty, followed by eight hours for him.)

Even the wife of one of his professors took a shift.

"I see this immediate emotional response to my plight as very human. So heartwarming." Tim always marveled at the great swell of compassion that constantly engulfed him.

By midlife, Tim's early views on money and possessions had consolidated. He described his life-situation as "comfortable," but really not much more. He had to budget carefully to pay his attendants adequately and to maintain his home. For him, money was always something

The newlyweds on their first journey home together to Cave Hill, Barbados

to be counted, not recklessly spent. So, what of the great spenders out there? Some of them may share Tim's profession but certainly not his heart. He has placed his values elsewhere. At first, his father's oft-repeated advice about the "houses and lands" that would keep people out of heaven conditioned Tim. Also, the years of coping with enormous problems channeled him into genuine non-materialism.

Twice his hydraulic lift at home failed. Needing repairs, it veered to the left and dumped Tim on the floor. Occasionally, over-tired attendants let him fall as they were strapping him to the tilt board. Invariably, he had the same response. "Get me up now. You can do it." Sometimes all he had was a couple of women standing by. "Go on. Do it." With the strength of his mind, it is a wonder that he didn't levitate himself off the floor and back into the chair himself.

Still, sitting upright in his chair all day took

much effort. "But I have my recreation waiting for me when I get home," Tim would say with a happy lift in his voice. "It's my standing board."

Standing, strapped to the board, Tim spent many pleasurable hours. The weight bearing helped prevent osteoporosis in the long bones and improved circulation. Fitted with a little desk-tray, he could read, write, and watch television. He also had plenty of time there to talk to his friends on the phone. Tim would almost glow with anticipation as he spoke of this "marvelous relaxation" awaiting him at home. Also, he had straps mounted over his bed so that he could do a hundred pull-ups morning and evening.

One man goes to the beach. Another jogs. Another plays golf—all for health, enjoyment, and exercise. Timothy Greaves' enthusiasm for his tilt board was touching. Perhaps it represented the vestigial remains of the energy he used to devote to playing cricket back in Trinidad.

Upon arrival at Loma Linda University Medical Center, Thelda Van Lange specialized in orthopedic nursing. Unknowingly, she was in training for the enormous responsibilities that marriage would bring to her.

It comes as no surprise that a person working with a major handicap would have a strong personality. Survival depends on it. Indeed, he may occasionally lapse over into anger and aggression. He simply cannot "suffer fools gladly."

As time went on, Tim attained a remarkable level of attitude adjustment. He, himself, trained his caregivers—be it parent, wife, or hired attendant. He figured out the most efficient ways for him to be moved on and off the bed, in and out of the wheelchair, and everything else.

He demanded that everything be done right. In his struggle to look after himself, he understood exactly his own needs and how to deal with them. Woe to the attendant who tried to deviate from his plan. He expected people to have common sense about his care and to do it the right way. Not for a moment did his attention lose focus. "You didn't wash your hands long enough," he'd bark. He never missed a detail.

The transfer in and out of the car looked

complicated, but Tim himself reduced it to a fine art. The arm of his wheelchair was lowered, and the attendant held his feet together and lifted them into the car first. Tim bowed his head forward while the beveled sliding board was pushed underneath him. With his braced right arm, he clung to the handle over the car door. His companion grasped him by the back of his pants and his belt. In one long, smooth move he was planted on the car seat. This could be done without a mechanical lift. He never sat back waiting for something to happen. He involved himself by doing everything he could possibly manage to promote his own cause.

So his workdays ended. From his office window, Tim looked out the window where the sun was setting in a hazy red glow,

From home at 1860 Via Del Rey, South Pasadena, Tim, with his attendant, Mervyn Alexander, leave for work at Los Angeles County Hospital. He had an "at-home" electric wheelchair. Upon arrival in the doctors' garage, his driver would transfer him to his "office chair."

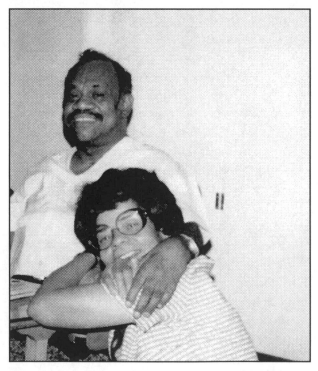

Tim and one of his favorite cousins, Pretha Boyce. At the time of the accident, she took off six weeks from her nursing duties in Glendale to care for him (thereby jeopardizing her own job).

a backdrop for thousands of busy, insect-like cars scurrying in and out and over the East Los Angeles freeway interchange. Then his attendant came to take him home.

Occasionally, Tim could also be astonishingly patient. Soon after their marriage, Thelda went shopping for a new china cabinet for their home. She hoped she had made the right choice, and she brought Tim in to help make the final decision.

The salesman ignored Tim, as if he were deaf, blind, and mute. Even when Tim chose a more expensive piece of furniture than Thelda had asked for, the man didn't acknowledge the wheelchair customer in any way.

Sometimes when they went out to dinner at a restaurant, the waiter would talk over Tim's head, never making eye contact with him. "What does he want?" Tim smoothly controlled all of his instincts to wrath.

One day, Tim sat quietly in a New York airport while his companions, Lindy Gallimore and Pretha Boyce, argued with the agent at the ticket counter. Negotiations did not go well. The agents insisted that their return tickets to California were invalid. "You have to purchase new tickets."

While Tim patiently explained the situa-

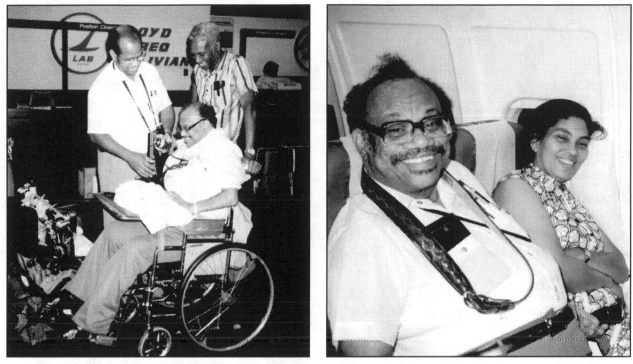

Forever in love with travel, Tim invented several smooth moves to get himself through an airport and on to the plane. Left. Helpers were always at hand. In this case in Miami Airport, Drs. Orville Roberts and Linbrook Barker attended him. Right. Tim and Thelda wait for the take-off that will set them down in Barbados.

tion, his cousin and Lindy couldn't even follow the argument. Tim, as usual, won.

Although they did not have to purchase new tickets, more was to come. Next—perhaps in retribution—the security guards searched Tim as if he were a card-carrying terrorist. They undid his braces, took off his shoes, and carried their investigations on to the point of the ridiculous.

When the Greaves finally boarded the flight, Tim remarked to Thelda, "Do they actually think that anyone would go to this extreme to disguise himself as a terrorist?"

Such encounters vexed Thelda intensely. Tim, on the other hand, was able to sit quietly in his wheelchair and tune out all of the nonsense and the rage. He knew, in an instant of time, how to reduce himself from aggressiveness to sheep-like submissiveness.

Chapter 8

Riding the Crest of the Wave

Tim had an unbounded interest in people. He was, so to speak, chronically sociable. He spent long hours on the telephone, where he offered wisdom but also demonstrated himself to be an excellent listener. People in his presence felt worthy of regard. Moreover, any secret confided to Tim was there to stay forever.

Tim himself, and later with Thelda, used his house as a kind of way station. All kinds of people came and went. For instance, as a teenager in Trinidad, he met a girl at Bates Memorial School where he taught for just six months. Almost 50 years later, that same lady followed him all the way to Cave Hill just to meet her old teacher. That visit happened on Tim's last trip home to Barbados.

One year-long guest was Marilyn Cathcart, Thelda's roommate from Hinsdale days. She lived with the Greaves while she worked on and off a cruise ship. (She and her sisters had become Thelda's "American family".) For their entertainment (and his), he took the ladies to several sporting events in the stadium with him. Also, once in a while, a Greek play. Such were his catholic tastes.

Tim would have loved to entertain even more guests at home. Indeed, from time to time, they had live-in people for months at a time. With her professional work and 24-hour caregiving, however, Thelda had to submit to her limitations.

Sometimes Tim had trouble remembering this fact of life.

The passion for giving back, for making a contribution, had been thoroughly embedded in Tim's psyche. "It was Caribbean Training College that really shaped my life," he insisted. "That's where my goals crystallized. It was a 'rite of passage' for me." Tim could never say enough about what that "little school" had done for him. "I have had my own success and security, so I must give other youth a chance." His assistance ranged from financial support to guiding them into academia, to keeping them in his own home. "A life without a cause is a life without effect" evolved into a major motif of Tim's life.

Even before his shattering accident, the seed of a huge idea had lodged in Tim's mind. Back in 1959, an article in the *Review & Herald* had

One of the plans closest to Tim Greaves' heart was the establishment of a Mayo-like clinic of medical specialists in Trinidad. Here (far right), he consulted with friends and colleagues about the projet for the South Caribbean. When the idea did not come to fruition, he suffered profound disappointment.

Left. Lindy Gallimore was Tim's medical school classmate, oftentimes attendant, and close friend. Tim thoroughly enjoyed the times when the irrepressible Lindy dropped in to share a joke or two. On this occasion, he clapped his own hat on Tim's head and then sat back to study the effect. Right. One day, with mutual pleasure, two young black men met at Lindy's home. Tim, the sports fan, met a star. Muhammed Ali became acquainted with a hero of another kind (about 1965).

caught his attention. It concerned medical work in Trinidad. Once that idea had burst out alive in his head, it never left him. As he worked on his dream project, he seemed to hardly factor in his personal limitations. Even at that early stage of his career, the idea possessed him.

His friends, his countrymen, and strangers—they all heard about it.

He envisioned a medical clinic in Trinidad run by homegrown Caribbean specialists. He gained the support of surgeons, cardiologists, dentists, and more. The physicians would have their own clinical setting and would be able to generate business for the hospital. Eventually, even the wives were persuaded to go on this great mission. More than one couple sold their homes in preparation for moving back to the Caribbean.

The group wrote up the proposal and prayed over it. When the project was laid before the Church administrators, however, it met with a dismaying reaction. The committee eyed the proposition with profound suspicion.

One of the plans closest to Tim Greaves' heart was the establishment of a Mayo-like clinic of medical specialists in Trinidad. Here he (far right) consulted with friends and colleagues about

the project for the South Caribbean. When the idea did not come to fruition, he suffered profound disappointment.

"What's wrong with these people?" the committee wanted to know. Who could explain why a bunch of practitioners would be willing to move back to the islands to provide medical services? Had they failed in their work in the United States? Did they want to come back now to Trinidad like whipped puppies and then make themselves to be the "big ones" at home?

So the committee stalled out. One cynic even asked, "After you've fleeced the hospital, then what will you think to do next?"

Tim realized that his plan could not materialize. The disappointment almost crushed him. At the same time, some of his dedicated friends had to invest in new real estate and restructure their medical practices.

Needing to recover from this grief, but still desiring to work for his own people, Tim asked for sabbatical leave from his work in Southern California. For more than a year (a very good year) Tim worked back home in Barbados.

Tim's inner compass, however, never allowed him to drift into political meanness. On one oc-

Left. Although he had no children of his own, Tim readily identified with other people's offspring—especially with his nephew, Baby Johann Andrews. Right. Johann had a lifelong attachment to his beloved Uncle Tim.

casion, Loma Linda University invited him out to the campus to talk about his student experience in the medical school. Unquestionably, it had been out of the ordinary.

Upon Tim's arrival, a black journalist accosted him. With one purpose in mind, the man pushed his way into the interview. He wanted to know if Tim had something negative to say about the white faculty who had worked with him. He baited him with well-prepared questions.

Taken aback, Tim stared at the reporter. Finally, the words came to him. "Now I am really disappointed that I took a day off work to come out here for such a purpose as this."

A flood of memories rushed into Tim's head. What about Dr. Harold Shryock who, during his residency, had invited Tim to be his reader? Plus the care of all of the rest of the faculty. To say nothing of his many classmates who came from every imaginable ethnic background. Never be unfair to any other person. Tim lived by this code.

"No. I have no complaints of that kind. None!" Tim sat stolidly waiting until the reporter finally dismissed himself.

That interview was never published.

By and large, Tim's professional work fell into a predictable pattern. He dictated to his secretary, Joy, who produced reports on slides along with his diagnoses. Near the end of his work years, he even learned to use a computer.

Undeniably, Tim had a fierce determination to have things his way. Therefore, life did not always run smoothly in the office. The staff would fall out and fall in again, as circumstances dictated. Still, they always loved him.

One day he wheeled in from another office, dropping a piece of blank paper on the floor. "Give me that paper," he demanded.

Seeing it was only paper, Joy offered him another sheet from her own desk. Tim flared up, glaring at the paper on the floor. He had made an effort to bring it in, and now it had escaped. All of that hard work! He refused to be insulted. "I want 'dat' paper," he growled.

He got it. That almost childish tantrum, however, offended Joy for days.

Usually his rage related to real blunders. When one of his histo-technicians accidentally exposed an entire roll of film, the two of them did not speak to one another for three months.

On the less-confrontational side, Tim had a lifetime addiction to news. Local, international, personal. Documentaries, newscasts, whatever. As soon as he arrived home, he wanted to mix into it immediately.

Nothing in the world around him, however,

stirred Tim more than sports. A throwback to his teenage athleticism, he remained very knowledgeable about cricket. But on taking up residence in the United States, he, perforce, had to transfer his devotion to football.

From time to time, friends took him to various sporting events. Otherwise, he drifted into comfortable evenings and weekends watching games on television with his friend, Dr. Herman Ricketts.

Sunday afternoon ball games on TV at Ricketts' house. This diversion gave the two friends some of the happiest interludes in their workweeks.

Comfortable? Not always! In tense moments, Tim would lapse into such stress over the condition of the Los Angeles Lakers that he couldn't bear to watch. "Just tell me what it is when it's over," he would plead. Then, when his heart palpitations had subsided, he could rejoin the spectators.

This passion for the game set Tim at the extreme end of emotional involvement, opposite to the lugubrious ones who have no interest in sports. Nor in little else, for that matter. This wheelchair doctor was simply born with endless curiosity and an unquenchable zest for life. Sports were only one of his many strong, but therapeutic, diversions.

In the first forty-two years of Super Bowl history, Rick and Tim shared every game, except for the two years that Ricketts served in the military. Indeed, the last time occurred during Tim's final hospitalization. The last game they shared was a win for the New Orleans Saints (2010). Later, Rick took whimsical comfort in the team's sport-victory song, "When the Saints Go Marching In." Tim was traveling in that direction too!

Given his super-active youth, more modified recreation made up Tim's post-accident years. At home, he could quickly become bored. Television and reading could occupy him only so long. He loved just to be out in the sunshine. Once retired, he insisted on going somewhere every day in the car.

Tim loved travel. He never stopped loving big travel. No matter the challenges and whoever had to cope with them, if there was something to see, he wanted to see it. Whenever he decided to go somewhere, more often than not, he went.

Of course, he managed a considerable amount of travel within the parameters of his work. Attending medical conventions, reading papers, and going to alumni meetings—these events took him over the length and breadth of the nation. His enthusiasm never waned: "Just let me do what I can do!"

On these occasions he savored the flavor of each city far beyond any scientific concerns. In New Orleans, he wheeled through the French

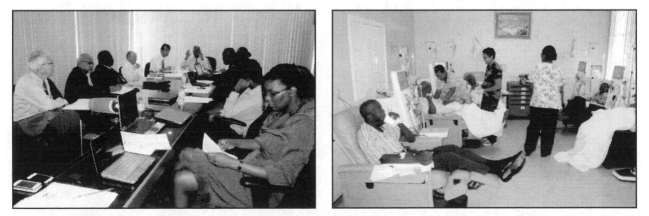

Left. One of the strongest links in Loma Linda University Medical Center and the Seventh-day Adventist Community Hospital in Trinidad has been Dr. Robert Soderblom (CME class of 1963). First at the left, Dr. Bob sits with the hospital board. Right. The dialysis unit in the new extension has been added to the improved facility in Trinidad. Tim Greaves would be pleased.

Tim never tired of seeing exotic sights, no matter how complicated the task of getting there. Left. Tim waited in the car, eager for the next stage of his and Thelda's tour of Western Canada. Right. Another time, he and Thelda posed on the wharf in Boston Harbor beside the reconstituted "Mayflower."

Quarter while eating Haagen-Dazs ice-cream. Unable to control the pressure of his two functional fingers, he couldn't handle a cone. As usual, when all else failed, he submitted to the necessity of using a dish. On the same excursion, he stopped and let the street shoe-shiners spit on his boots and polish them for him—those handsome, lovingly cared-for boots that never walked.

Wheelchair notwithstanding, Tim often had the last word in travel events. Upon returning from a business seminar in the Caribbean, Thelda and their friend, Juanita Boyd, were impatiently searching for their luggage on the carousel. A voice from behind them remarked, "It's there. In fact, it has already gone by twice!"

The women seized the bags on the third round. From the disadvantaged back row, Tim's two eyes had seen what their four eyes had missed. Tim never changed!

He also took every opportunity to attend General Conference sessions of his Church, wherever they happened to be. Also, they took home journeys to the Caribbean at fairly frequent intervals.

Beyond these more-or-less-functional journeys lay exotic adventures that he strategized

for himself. Pure recreation. In his early student days, he had visited the Canadian Rockies. Later, he determined to see Western Canada again. He wanted Thelda to see it too.

In 2003, Tim got fired up with an even more adventurous idea. His graduating class of 1963 was taking an ocean cruise in Australia and New Zealand. When the plan exploded before her one night, Thelda truly felt that the trip was beyond her capability to manage him successfully. She didn't have long, however, to worry about the matter. Nothing but possibilities filled Tim's range of view.

After the last day for signing up had passed, Tim did sign up. "We're going to Australia," he crowed as he wheeled through the front door a few days later.

Thereafter, they basked in the luxuries of the cruise ship, visited Sydney's Opera House, and all similar destinations. Also Tasmania, and historic Avondale College. The main attractions did not, however, fulfill all of Tim's desires. Nor did the tour buses provide wheelchair accommodations. Therefore, he hired taxis to take him and Thelda to other places like two important cricket pitches (playing fields) in Sydney and Melbourne. As he

Herman Ricketts and Tim Greaves has so many things in common. Both were Caribbean islanders. Both physicians. Both were alumni of the College of Medical Evangelists and share the same friends, classmates, and church interests. They lived as near-neighbors in South Pasadena. Also, both were avid sports fans and enjoyed an equal passion for watching televised weekend games.

Tim loved to be anywhere that people were gathering and talking.

looked at the empty sports fields, he relished his favorite sport intellectually.

In New Zealand, amid the land- and ocean-scapes, gardens, and sheep paddocks, Tim observed a Maori gardener staring at him intently. Surely his wheelchair was not that much of a novelty. "What's that about, do you think?" Tim speculated.

Thelda smiled. "Look at him," she prompted. "You look just like him. He wonders, probably, why you're a tourist riding around in a taxi."

To the very end, Tim could never get enough. When he wanted to see London and then travel through Europe, however, Thelda held firm. Exhausted herself, she just could not manage the "grand tour." Such a trip would take them through non-wheelchair-friendly territory with high curbs, cobblestone streets, and so forth.

Unaware of his own failing strength, he told Thelda, "We could just go anyway." He added, "We can easily pay for it now. Why are you holding back?"

"No, Tim, it was not about money," Thelda replied. She looked down at him sadly. How could she find a way to tell him that, age, both his and hers, does heavy damage to bodies. It happens while the spirit still soars high.

When Tim died in 2010, Thelda discovered that he had made arrangements with his brother, Donn, to travel with him to Europe the next year. The plot had been carefully laid. So that was Tim's last word on the subject of travel and seeing the world.

Chapter 9

Approaching a Destination

"I am crucified with Christ; nevertheless I live; yet not I, but Christ liveth in me: And the life which I now live in the flesh I live by the faith of the Son of God, who loved me and gave himself for me." Galatians 2:20 (Timothy Greaves' favorite text).

Retirement from his work at Los Angeles Country Hospital and his professorship at the University of Southern California did not come easily for Tim Greaves. This, despite the fact that he had a lovely home with Thelda, that he had countless numbers of friends, and that he had devised all kinds of activities for himself. For fifty years, his laboratories had been his second home. He always gave maximum service and often worked overtime. Not surprisingly, his staff became a second family.

Naturally, his colleagues wanted an enormous retirement party. Tim, however, recalled the mega-celebration they had given him when he returned from his fifteen-month sabbatical in Barbados. That time, he found a huge banner draped across the entrance to the pathology department: "Welcome Home TSG." Inside, a big festive event awaited him.

Never wanting to be center stage, Tim always looked out rather than in. So he begged: "Please don't do it. I really don't want a party." They respected his wishes—at least for the time being.

Later, as Tim's seventy-fifth birthday approached, his cousin Eunice Boyce had a proposal. "Let's make a surprise Thanksgiving celebration for his seventy-fifth birthday." So, under the guise of honoring a friend's birthday (which was the same day as Tim's), plans went forward. Fully aware of his reluctance ever to be an object of attention, the ladies had to rationalize.

"After all, God has really blessed him with a long life. That's worthy of celebration. It's the right thing to do." Friends went to work.

Upon arrival at the restaurant, Tim subsided into dour shock. But only at first. After the celebration ended, Tim told Thelda, "I thought something was afoot, but I couldn't figure it out." For someone who always wanted to know, this constituted a major defeat.

As expected, the loving warmth that pervaded the room enveloped him. Tim's many, many friends demanded the privilege of honoring him in the way that they wished. So they had their way.

As it turned out, the timing of that seventy-fifth birthday party was exactly right. Indeed, they had only a two-week window of time in which to accomplish their purpose.

Ever since his retirement in March, 2008, Tim had been doing volunteer work three days a week in his lab. He could never find enough to do just staying at home. Inert as he was, he aimed to get out of the house every day. With his old stubborn resolve, he forced his worn-out body to keep pace with his brilliant mind that, as always, soared in full flight.

Like other volunteers, Tim had to sign certain official papers each year in order to be approved for volunteer work. When he applied in January of 2010, he was pleased to be accepted once more. That year, however, he was able to go to his laboratory for just one day.

It's often difficult to identify the precise moment when a life begins its final decline. With the advantage of hindsight, Thelda feels that it started for Tim about ten years earlier. From then on, he began having frequent bladder infections. Surrounded by physician friends (specialists of all kinds), Tim had access to the best care. Indeed, he himself was there among them, quite able to monitor himself and consult about preferred treatments. After a while, the antibiotics became

Tim loved, above all, to be in the middle of things. It could be Niagara Falls or his own back yard. No matter. Paradoxically, he never wanted anyone making a fuss over him.

stronger and stronger, and, at the same time, less effective. By 2009, Tim was in almost constant difficulty. He patronized the nearby large (635-bed) Huntington Memorial Hospital in Pasadena quite often.

The potential for lethal illnesses exists in every human being. Then, with age, comes the possibility of the door opening a little wider and allowing disease to rush in upon us. Sometimes that moment can be traced to a single event that serves as a triggering device.

In December, 2009, Tim and Thelda made what would be their last trip home together to Barbados and Trinidad. In January, they had a stopover in Miami, Florida.

Thelda bought a meal in the airport that suited their vegetarian preferences—tofu curry. Then, just as they were about to eat, the loudspeaker crackled alive. Their departure gate had been changed. As she had done so many times before, Thelda made the race through the concourse, pushing Tim's chair and trying to beat the clock. Once aboard, they shared the food and then settled into the flight to Los Angeles.

In due course, they arrived home, but all was not well. As they reached their front door, Thelda suddenly vomited in the entryway. While Tim waited, she cleaned up the floor. Then she was sick again. The next afternoon, Friday, she went grocery shopping and prepared for guests at lunch the next day. Still sick, she went on retching through the following night.

Although Tim fell ill on Saturday night, it was Monday morning before he could say the words: "Thelda, you'd better take me to the emergency room." He knew that he had more things to worry about than mere dehydration. Moreover, it had a world-class trauma center. Tim was admitted for three days.

He returned home with the usual gratitude that any patient feels upon being released from hospital. As desperately as he wanted to get well, one more time, he knew better. From then on, however, Tim spiraled downward. "I just don't feel well."

While Thelda recovered from the bout of food poisoning, for Tim it was the beginning of the end. Within two weeks, he returned to Huntington Memorial, once again in the hands of his skilled physicians. His attendants at the hospital often praised him: "Yes, we know what we're doing now. That's because you are the one who taught us pathology!"

Tim's ever-active brain worked in high gear virtually to the end. "I never took a class from him," one ENT doctor at Rancho Los Amigos who had never met him before said. "But I wish I had. Everyone remembers what a very bright physician he was. As he still is, I see."

Something happened on one of Tim's later hospital days that brightened his spirits immensely. The president of the University of the Southern Caribbean visited him. "We are giving you an honorary doctorate," he said.

The announcement had arrived just in time.

Above. Tim Greaves' seventh-fifth birthday. Thelda wheeled him into the Castaway Restaurant, Burbank, a favorite meeting place for Caribbean friends. Right: Despite his astonishment, Tim rallied and made a forceful speech. He would not even let Thelda hold the microphone for him. Above right. Jolly cousins soon set the pace for the party. From left. Pat Stoll, Thelda Greaves, Lloyd Stoll, Zena Stoll-Bone, and Fred Bone.

When Herman Ricketts visited in the hospital, he found Tim as happy as a dog with two tails. "Hey, man! Guess what!" Tim's smile stretched from ear to ear. "You know, Rick, the University of the Southern Caribbean is giving me an honorary degree! Think of that!"

To be sure, Tim didn't lack degrees and awards. Not at all! This recognition, however, came from a place that was invisible to most observers. Within the University of the Southern Caribbean, at its heart, lay the foundational remains of Caribbean Training College. Sixty years earlier, that little old school had set Tim firmly on his life's pathway. The prospect thrilled him in a way he had probably never experienced.

Although Tim would never hold the plaque in his hands, its significance spoke directly to his spirit.

From the start, Dr. Herman Ricketts (cardiologist), had, however, became anxious from the first time Tim entered Huntington with food poisoning. He had "coded" (cardiac arrest) soon after his arrival. "I am pretty sure," Rick said, "that Tim won't survive this time. His case is very complicated."

"I know," his wife Pansy replied. "He has been to the edge so many times, but it's still hard for anyone to believe that he won't fight it off again." When they reached his bedside, however, they found the usual old Tim, alert and very upbeat.

Shortly, they went out for a quick lunch. They had just finished their meal, however, when Pansy's cell phone rang. A clinical voice announced, "Dr. Greaves has coded again. We

Left. Tim's handsome, youthful portrait stands in pride of place, in the house where his wife Thelda still lives. Right. Tim at the end of the road with this, his last more-or-less "well" picture—his face sensitive and cheerful as always. His colleagues wrote: "Our lives have been that much better for having shared space and time with him."[1] They made no mention of his handicap. It simply did not matter.

1 Sara Reeve, Obituary, *HSC Weekly,* 2010-05-28.

thought you should know."

As they walked back to the hospital, Rick mused, "As I said, how can he make it? Not with his physical condition, age, and diagnoses!"

That same day, Tim coded a third time. The Ricketts stayed with him in ICU until well after midnight. As they left, Pansy whispered, "I'm sure we won't see him alive again after tonight."

How wrong they were! Two months later, Tim was transferred to the Rancho Los Amigos Rehabilitation Center, a familiar place from the early days of his paralysis.

From the beginning of the final months of hospitalization, the Ricketts regarded this survival of one of their best friends as a miracle, a

metaphor of Tim's entire life. A miracle because each living day was wholly unexpected. It seemed to be made up of two ingredients—God's mercy and Tim's determination not to leave one minute sooner than necessary.

Nonetheless, he coded again the day he arrived at Los Amigos. One of his pathology colleagues visited him. "You do understand the implications of repeated cardiac arrest, Tim. Do you really want to be resuscitated?"

Without an instant's hesitation, the patient replied in his usual powerful voice. "Oh, yes!"

Moments later Pansy arrived with the same question. "What do you want us to do if you code again, Tim?"

Above left. On May 23, 2010, a large memorial service for Dr. Timothy Greaves was held in the Vallejo Drive Church, Glendale, California.[1] Above right. Always full of ideas, Tim was devoted to two concepts: Smart grooming and helping others. His family elected to send the contents of his personal closet to Africa. One pastor stands among the luggage holding shirts and ties. Right. Another displays a shiny pair of Tim's boots. He will take them walking for the first time. They have never done that before.

1 The department of pathology at Los Angeles County Hospital/University of Southern California sponsored the first memorial service for Dr. Greaves. His colleagues (many of them in tears) filled the room—to standing room only. Other memorial services for Dr. Timothy S. Greaves were held in New York and Barbados.

"Bring me back." Tim stared up at her, a glint in his eye. "Every time!" Pansy looked at their dear companion. Friends for more than fifty years, she realized that she had never known a person more in love with living than Tim Greaves.

One of his friends was on staff as a surgeon at Huntington. Tim and George Williams (of Guyana) had been students together at CTC back in Trinidad. Now the two of them had to enter into the sad, end-of-life intimacies.

George's devotion had a long backstory. By the time he arrived in Loma Linda, part of Tim's family had returned to Barbados. Behind in payments and needing to live outside of the dormitory, George quickly found himself part of the Greaves household. He was given a corner of the little house on Mound Street, the one where Tim, his brother, Donn, and their mother lived. He stayed for two years! "Of course, I helped," George will tell you. "But they respected my medical school study load and spared me most of the heavy lifting."

"It has always been a two-way street for George and me," Tim declared, more than once.

While Tim's final crisis proved to be cardiac, George felt that the many blood transfusions he had received at the time of the accident had compromised his liver. The Hepatitis C (cirrhosis of the liver) had lain mainly dormant for decades, but finally it moved in as part of the last strike.

When Tim arrived at his last stopping place, Kindred Hospital, however, he did not have any acquaintances. There, in his third month of hospitalization, he virtually moved into hospice care. "He's the best patient I have ever seen," one of the doctors told Thelda. "He is so at peace. So cooperative. So calm."

Thelda, herself, had long ago told Tim what an excellent patient he was. And that, it should be noted, is a true accomplishment for any man. To say nothing of any husband. And, beyond that, any physician!

During those days, the grand old warrior slept a great deal, while Thelda and many others came to his bedside. At the beginning of the last illness, Tim had confessed to some of his friends, "I don't think I will make it this time." At the last,

the man who always needed to know did in fact understand. Thinking—mistakenly—that he was sparing his wife, he never shared this prognosis with her. This masculine inclination to withdraw from the nearest, dearest people in one's life, adds even more pain to the parting days. That part of the journey he did not understand.

Therefore, Thelda, in her customary direct connection with her God, believed to Tim's very last hour that her husband would still elude death. Yes, she had always prayed that His will be done. Yet within that parameter, she ardently hoped—believed—that God's will would be that Tim should live. Surely, one who gave so much, who was beloved by so many, and who so much wanted to live could be spared! For Thelda, therefore, the end came as a piercing, painful surprise. Only her faith could carry her through the next grievous steps she had to take.

On Friday afternoon, May 7, 2010, she sat

Left. Thelda Greaves stood by the niche containing the remains of her husband of twenty-nine years (Forest Lawn Memorial Park, Hollywood Hills, Los Angeles). Right. In matters of death as well as life, Thelda has had the unwavering support of family and dear friends. Her first cousin (and Tim's medical school roommate), Dr. Lloyd Stoll, stood beside her at the end and beyond. Alone, yet not alone.

by Tim's bed swabbing his dry mouth. (He had been taken off fluids.) Was he in sleep or coma? Who knew?

Suddenly he opened his eyes and smiled at her. A bright, happy smile. "It was so fresh, clean, and pure," she remembers. "So young and childlike." Then he lapsed again into sleep.

Having sat with him all through the previous night, she whispered, "I am going home now to take a nap. Do you understand, Tim?" Although he made no visible response, Thelda still felt convinced that they had connected in some immeasurable way. She turned back one more time: "I just have to leave you in God's hands, Dear One."

When she returned, the medical staff told her that they had coded him three times.

At 1:15 p.m., Dr. Timothy Greaves died. Thelda looked down on the same very relaxed and peaceful face that had smiled at her so joyously the day before. Surely he had seen something not yet visible to her.

So, that Sabbath afternoon, the sun set on Tim Greaves' faded horizon for the last time. Thelda knew she would never forget the intensity of that final conscious interaction she had with her husband. What a gloriously happy moment! What an incomparable gift!

The next day (May 9, 2010) one more significant event transpired. The University of the Southern Caribbean (formerly Caribbean Training College) awarded Tim an honorary doctorate. The old school had done much for him. In return, he had given much to his *alma mater*. His brother, Dr. Donn Greaves, received the diploma for him.

Thus the combination of death and the honor created two consecutive days that saturated everyone with the full range of human emotion.

At first, simple correspondence linked Tim and Thelda. Reserved though they both were (on both sides), the letters arrived steadily. Using CME letterhead, Tim could then write with an even hand. (Better, indeed, than one might expect from a would-be physician.) Letter-writing, however, proved to be only the beginning. The various bonds of love developed and tied the together over the long years. In the end, the evidence came in: there never *had* been anyone else for either of them.

Chapter 10

His Gift List

Without question, Timothy Greaves left a powerful legacy, derived from his determination to "make a difference." Beyond his love for people and his craving to be among them, he remained amazingly self-effacing. He would never have approved of the writing of his story. Were he alive today, he probably would feel that this biography had gone altogether too far. He would be surprised at the value we place on the gifts he gave us. "You mean that episode was that important?"

More than twenty years passed before he could even bring himself to give an interview that would put his life in perspective. When his story was first told thirty years ago,[1] the publishers asked for a little book that would be small enough to give away free. (Something to pick up in a doctor's office.) It would be a story about a man overcoming overwhelming physical disabilities. About keeping faith in horrendously difficult circumstances. About assuming responsibility. So went the narrative at that time.

Tim, however, was one of a kind—physically, intellectually, and spiritually. No pat answers ever applied in his case. The telling of his more complete story became a project for the fiftieth anniversary of his graduating class (1963). A proper kind of recognition for one of Loma Linda University's distinguished alumni.

Now that Tim has finished his course, we find that he demonstrated to us a great deal more than a strong will and physical endurance. His gift list is a long one. Out of it, we may distill at least seven traits that he modeled exceptionally well.

Tim's parents, Eric and Evelyn Greaves, taught him the grace of gratitude. Their devotion to his well-being also inspired his intense sense of loyalty.

Gratitude

Probably, there was not a day in his adult life that Tim did not acknowledge, at some level, gratitude for the people who had given so much of themselves for his success and comfort. High on the list were his parents, his extended family, and countless devoted friends. To say nothing of his wife, Thelda, who never left his side from the day they married.

Tim discovered that to be grateful for what he had was to be truly alive! He lived accordingly.

Humor

Laughter was a medicine that Tim often prescribed for himself and others. Sometimes,

---

1 Dorothy Minchin-Comm, *His Compassions Fail Not* (Washington DC: Review & Herald Pub. Assn., 1982), 31 pages.

lesser people make their way through life "enjoying poor health." They manage to wear out their caregivers and drive their friends to the point of exhaustion. Everyone has known a few of them. Not for one moment, however, did Tim ever "cash in" on victimhood. His cheerfulness, sense of humor, and self-possession bespoke almost perfect adjustment.

With his very creative ability to cope, people easily assumed that Tim, somehow, had it all made. Not exactly. "People tend to go on about their own lives, assuming that my life is a success story that's all written," he used to say, "as if my case were a closed file. But it is not. The struggle never ends. Each morning I have to begin again." When he opened his eyes each sunrise, he had to determine anew to make that day count.

Passing years never made him any less vulnerable. "I couldn't take anything for granted." In other words, he could not afford to be a pessimist.

Spirituality

Knowing that God had intervened directly in his life kept Tim firmly grounded spiritually. Thus he always had hope within his reach.

He once confessed to his wife: "Every day I try to move my legs. Every day." As if the force of his mind could recover muscular life after decades of decline! Indeed, he developed a will that seemed to have no limits.

In a different part of his brain, however, another fantasy visited him almost every night. "It is a strange thing!" He would shake his head in puzzlement. "You know when I dream, I am never in the wheelchair. I'm always running and walking—doing the old things in the old way." He wondered whether that meant that, subconsciously, he had never really accepted his handicap. "Consciously, I believe that I have, but …." His voice trailed away.

Is it too much to say that perhaps those dreams also point forward to a time when Tim really will walk again? Maybe they are fragments of hope and faith as much as they are the residue of frustration. Tim's all-time favorite hymn said it all. It describes a scientist who has found his faith:

> My faith has found a resting place;
> I need no other evidence.
>
> Not in a man-made creed;
> I need no other plea:
>
> I trust the ever-living One,
> It is enough that Jesus died;
>
> That he for me will plead.
> And rose again for me.[2]

Discipline

Tim approached his work with an accuracy and totality that resembled throwing a switch. Instant action! His eternal craving for intellectual activity was amply supplied by his work, as well by the awards he accrued from his varied achievements. Some came out of his ethnic background[3] while oth-

**Tim and Thelda at home
in Cave Hill Church, Barbados**

---

2 *Seventh-day Adventist Hymnal*, No. 523.
3 Alumnus of the Year, Caribbean Union College, Trinidad (1975); award from West Indies College, Jamaica; an honorary doctorate, University of the Southern Caribbean, Trinidad (2010). The University of the Southern Caribbean developed in three stages. CTC (Caribbean Training College) was followed by Caribbean Union College, and ultimately the college attained university status. The institution has several alumni chapters: In New Jersey, Florida (two), Atlanta, Alabama, New York, Washington, D.C., and Toronto, Canada. Also in Barbados and other

Of Courage, Compassion, and Endurance

Tim stoically regards his arm brace. The device liberated him to eat, to brush his teeth, and to manipulate the telephone. With effort he could even write—clumsily, but effectively.

ers derived from his academic connections.[4]

Both of his medical school classes recognized him. The one he dropped out of (1961) and the one with which he graduated (1963). In 1975 Loma Linda University's Honored Alumnus Award went to Timothy Greaves at its postgraduate convention banquet. He had attended other relatively ordinary class reunions, but this one exploded into fanfare.

Was he surprised? "I was shocked! I couldn't imagine who would put my name in for such an award!" His colleagues, on the other hand, could understand the reason why, even if Tim himself could not admit to it.

The many abuses his body suffered, of course, aged him. Still, the luster of his mind and heart never, in all of his seventy-five years, diminished.

Generosity

Tim created a new kind of self-sufficiency that was all his own. This complex achievement enabled him to give others much in return. Because of his passionate love for people, his life had, inevitably and forever, enmeshed with the lives of many people—all of them very emotionally involved in his battles.

With his attendants he was generous. They learned the meaning of loyal service. Webster Brown, for instance, served Tim and his circle of friends to the end. Today, he continues to go far beyond the end. Tim repeatedly opened wide his home to needy foreign students who could give little in return.

Balance

Tim did balance his professional life with recreation. Travel, socializing, and sports enlarged his world continually. It took much stamina for anyone to keep up with him.

At the same time, his energy so far exceeded his limitations that it took constant monitoring to

Tim with his long-time attendant, Webster Brown

Caribbean islands. At the time of his death, Dr. Greaves was president of the Southern California Chapter of USC.

4 The University of Southern California appointed him "Teacher of the Year" in the pathology department.

be sure that his plans did not drift off into the realm of the impossible and fantasy. The fire within him could hardly be controlled.

Fire

The pathology department at LAC/USC featured this picture of Dr. Timothy Greaves (bottom right photo) when it held its own, private memorial service for him. Suitably, the photograph was taken in his office.

Though accidental, the pose suggests a symbolic interpretation. It seems to say something profound about Tim. No device has yet been invented to quench the kind of fires that blazed in Tim's mind and heart.

❧❧❧❧❧

Tim's lively, inquiring mind, his compassion, his faith, and all of the rest of his loves bypassed his quadriplegia. Actually, the mobility of the average, healthy person becomes quite ordinary when compared to the distance Tim traveled beyond his limitations.

Indeed, God had said, "Yes, Tim, you will have your life. You will survive. But henceforth you must learn to live it in such a unique way that your gifts will light up your entire world."

And so he did.

Tim's passion for adventure matched his dedication to his work. Sometimes Thelda became involved in projects with which she could barely cope. Nonetheless, she measured up—most of the time.

Dr. Timothy Greaves (January 16, 1935-May 8, 2010) and the fire extinguisher

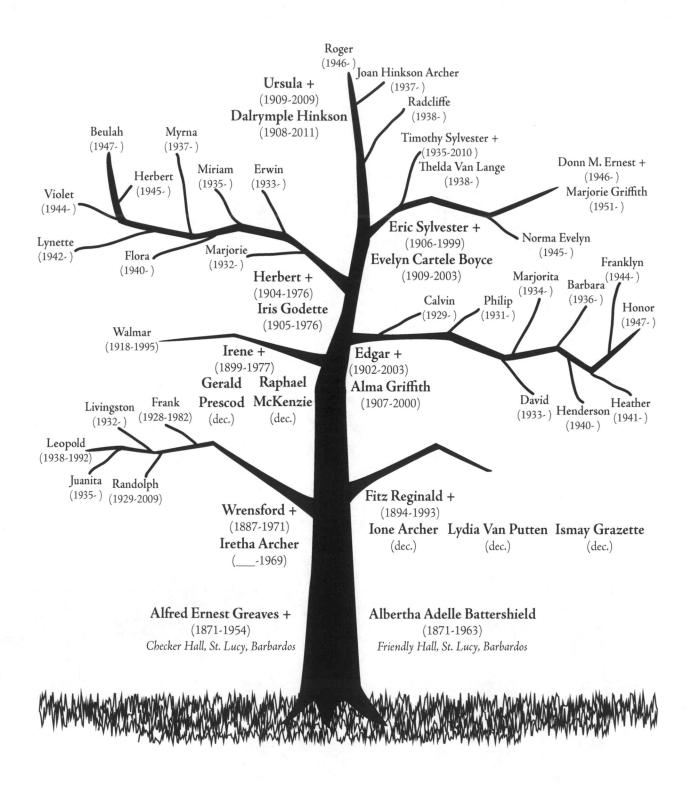

Roger
(1946-)

Joan Hinkson Archer
(1937-)

Ursula +
(1909-2009)
Dalrymple Hinkson
(1908-2011)

Radcliffe
(1938-)

Timothy Sylvester +
(1935-2010)

Thelda Van Lange
(1938-)

Donn M. Ernest +
(1946-)

Marjorie Griffith
(1951-)

Beulah
(1947-)

Myrna
(1937-)

Miriam
(1935-)

Erwin
(1933-)

Herbert
(1945-)

Violet
(1944-)

Eric Sylvester +
(1906-1999)
Evelyn Cartele Boyce
(1909-2003)

Norma Evelyn
(1945-)

Lynette
(1942-)

Flora
(1940-)

Marjorie
(1932-)

Herbert +
(1904-1976)
Iris Godette
(1905-1976)

Franklyn
(1944-)

Marjorita
(1934-)

Barbara
(1936-)

Honor
(1947-)

Calvin
(1929-)

Philip
(1931-)

Walmar
(1918-1995)

Irene +
(1899-1977)
**Gerald   Raphael
Prescod   McKenzie**
(dec.)   (dec.)

Edgar +
(1902-2003)
Alma Griffith
(1907-2000)

David
(1933-)

Henderson
(1940-)

Heather
(1941-)

Livingston
(1932-)

Frank
(1928-1982)

Leopold
(1938-1992)

Juanita
(1935-)

Randolph
(1929-2009)

Fitz Reginald +
(1894-1993)

Wrensford +
(1887-1971)
Iretha Archer
(____-1969)

Ione Archer
(dec.)

Lydia Van Putten
(dec.)

Ismay Grazette
(dec.)

Alfred Ernest Greaves +
(1871-1954)
Checker Hall, St. Lucy, Barbardos

Albertha Adelle Battershield
(1871-1963)
Friendly Hall, St. Lucy, Barbardos

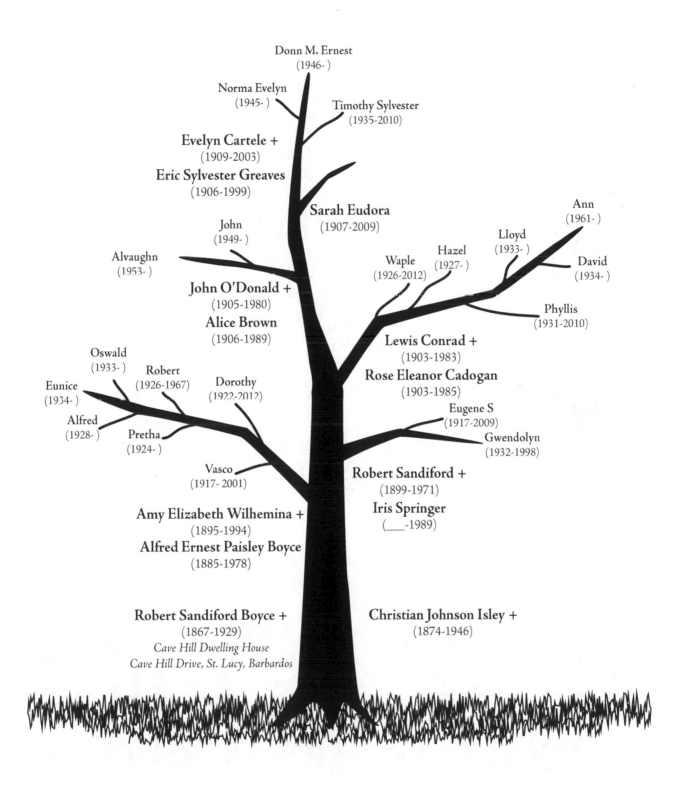

Donn M. Ernest
(1946-)

Norma Evelyn
(1945-)

Timothy Sylvester
(1935-2010)

Evelyn Cartele +
(1909-2003)
Eric Sylvester Greaves
(1906-1999)

Sarah Eudora
(1907-2009)

Ann
(1961-)

John
(1949-)

Lloyd
(1933-)

Alvaughn
(1953-)

Waple
(1926-2012)

Hazel
(1927-)

David
(1934-)

John O'Donald +
(1905-1980)
Alice Brown
(1906-1989)

Phyllis
(1931-2010)

Lewis Conrad +
(1903-1983)
Rose Eleanor Cadogan
(1903-1985)

Oswald
(1933-)

Robert
(1926-1967)

Dorothy
(1922-2012)

Eunice
(1934-)

Eugene S
(1917-2009)

Alfred
(1928-)

Pretha
(1924-)

Gwendolyn
(1932-1998)

Vasco
(1917- 2001)

Robert Sandiford +
(1899-1971)
Iris Springer
(___-1989)

Amy Elizabeth Wilhemina +
(1895-1994)
Alfred Ernest Paisley Boyce
(1885-1978)

Robert Sandiford Boyce +
(1867-1929)
Cave Hill Dwelling House
Cave Hill Drive, St. Lucy, Barbardos

Christian Johnson Isley +
(1874-1946)